Gratitude is a transformative force that connects us with the abundance of the universe. When we are grateful, we attract more reasons to be grateful and our lives are enriched in every way. Gratitude to God, for everything!

Dedicated to my little mermaid
Alice!

Golinha
2024

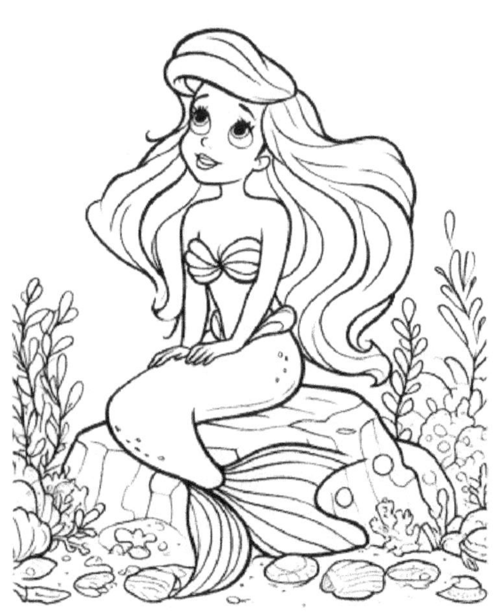 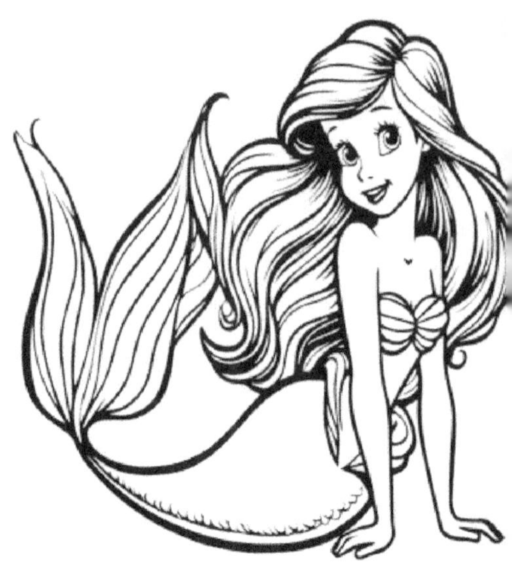

This Book Belongs to:

____

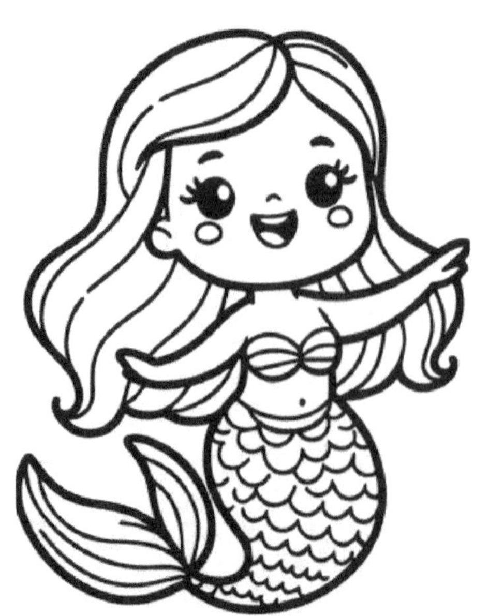 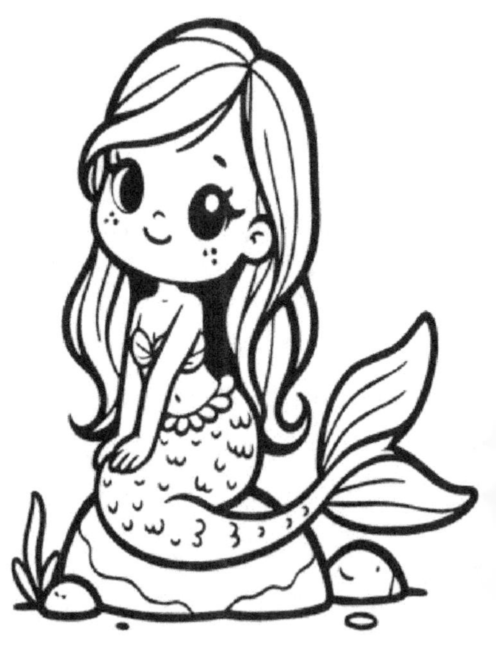

Test Color Page

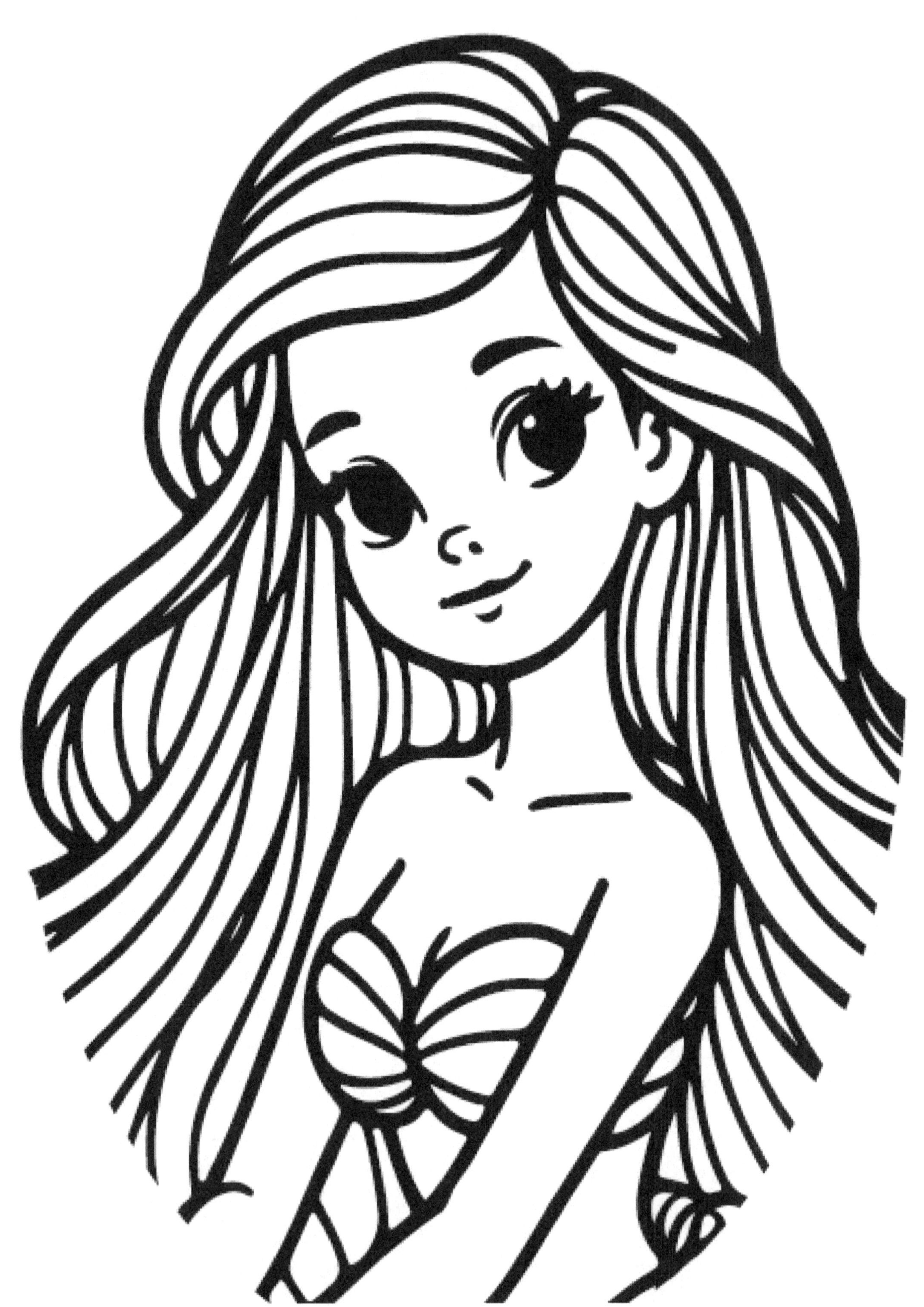

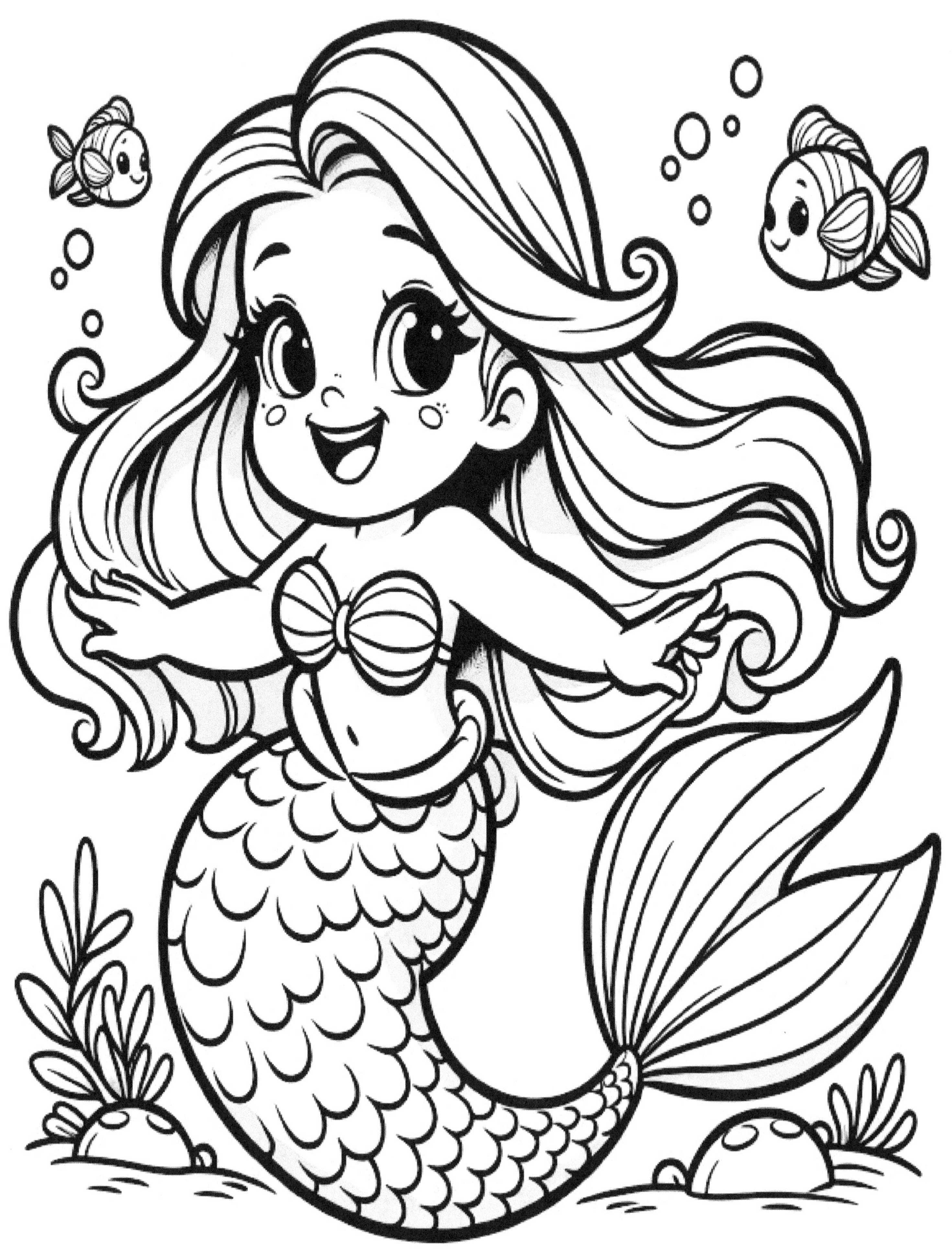

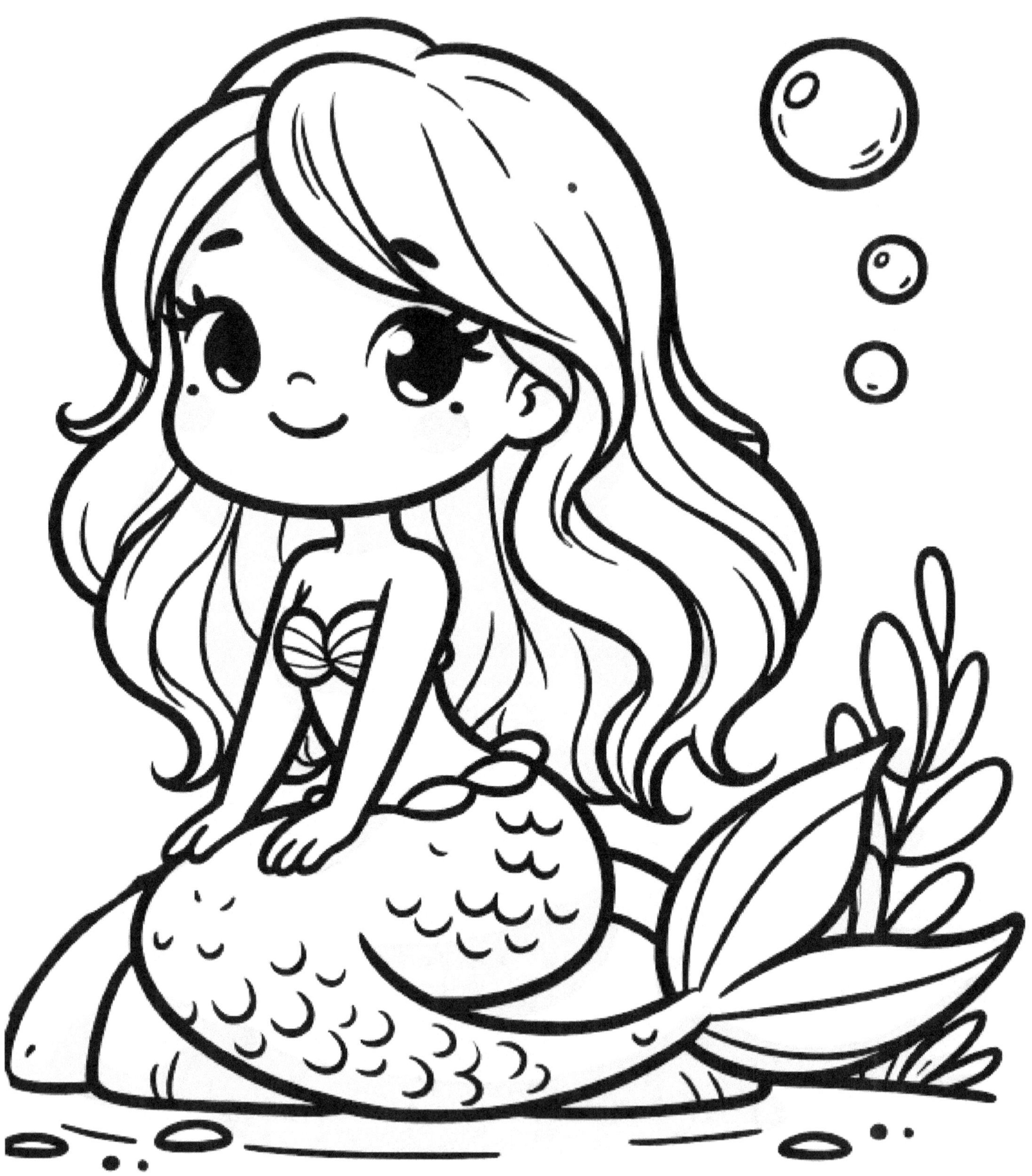

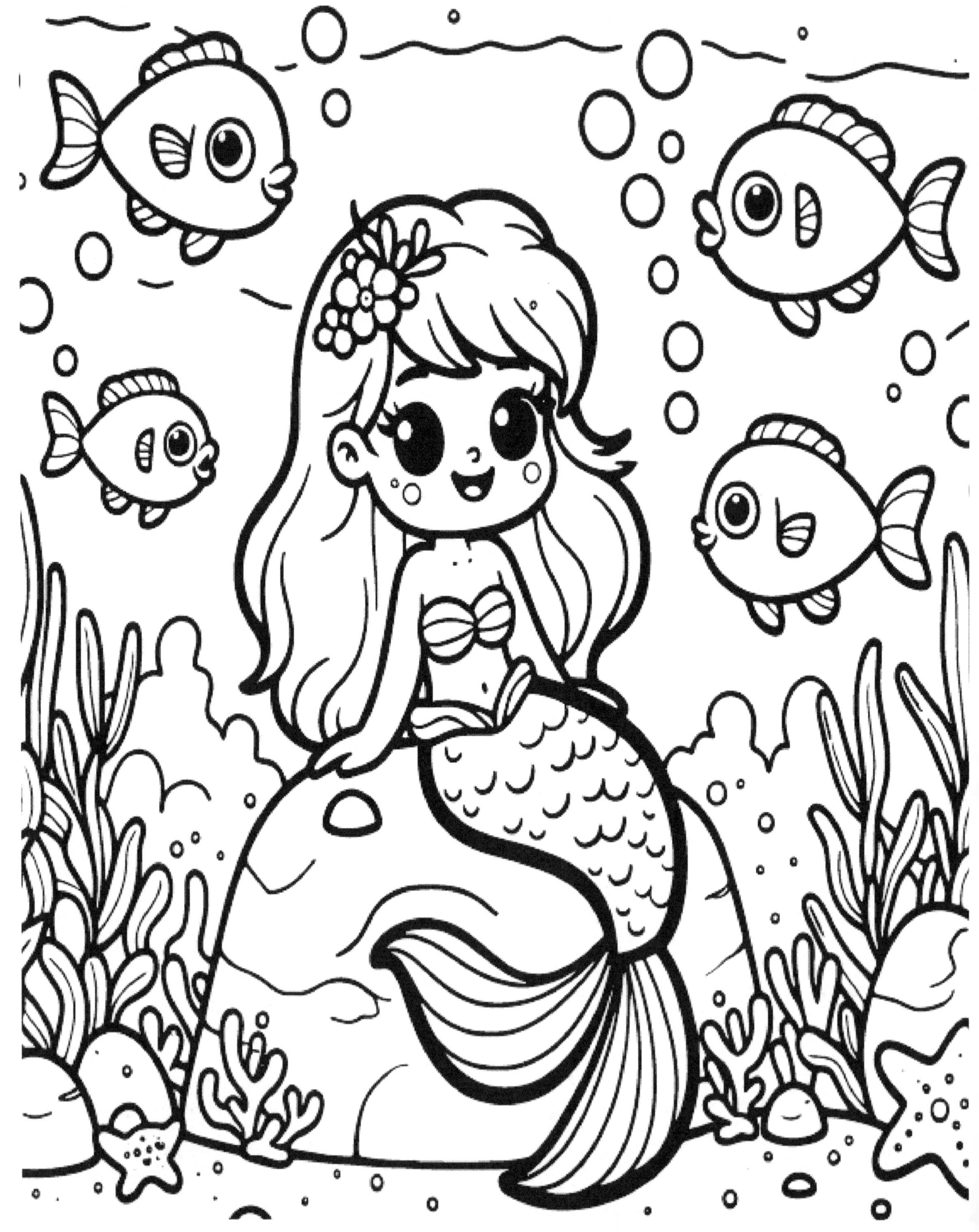

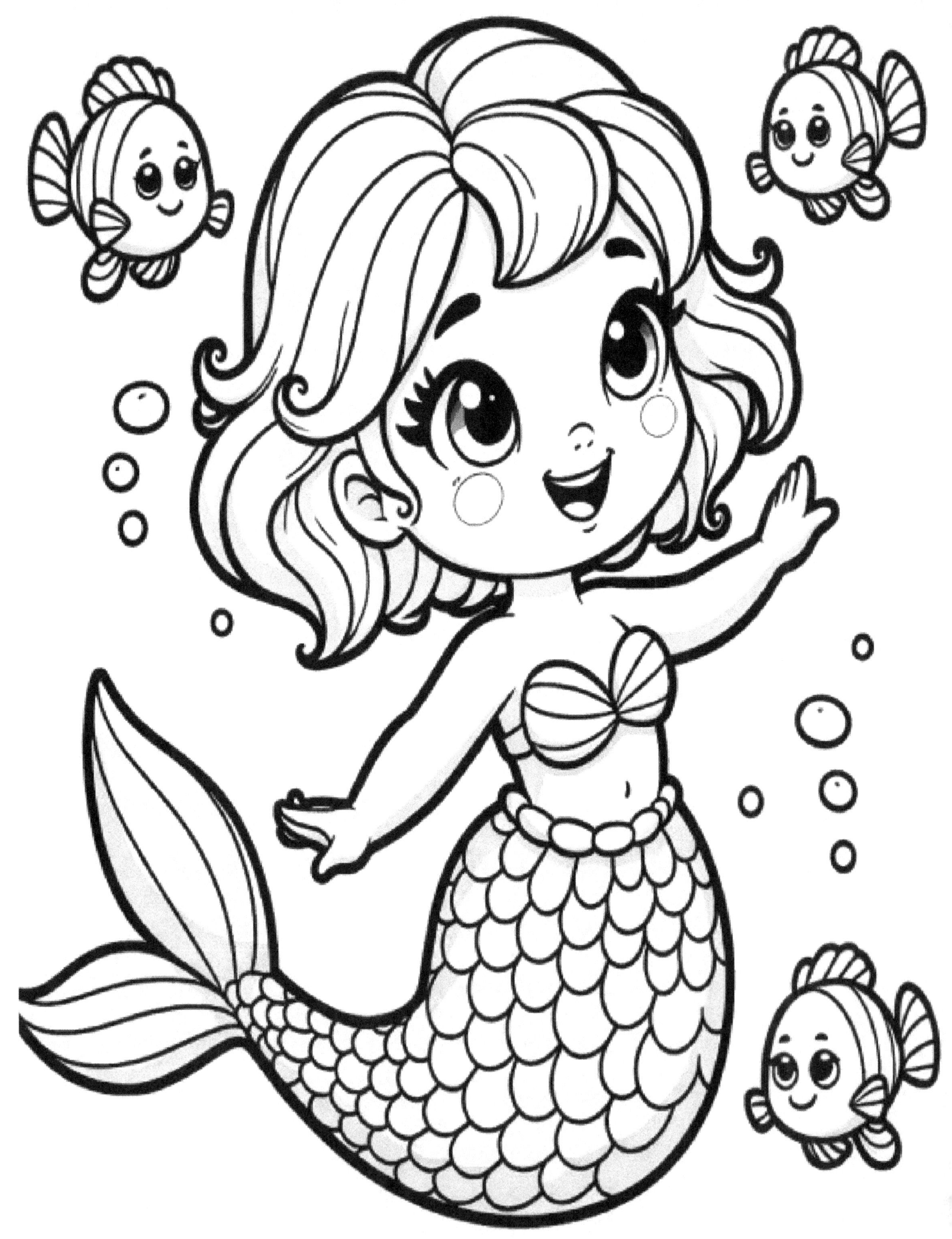

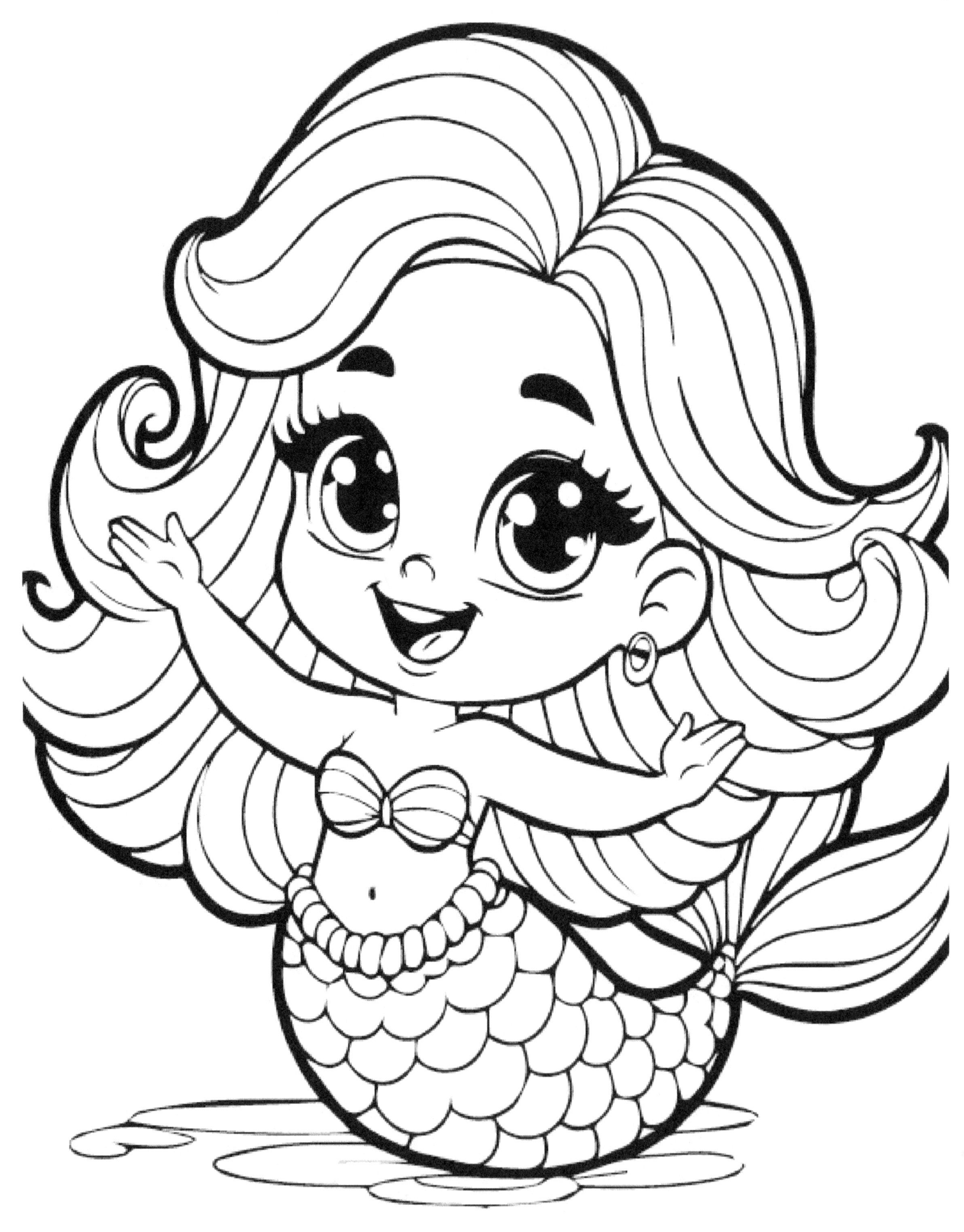

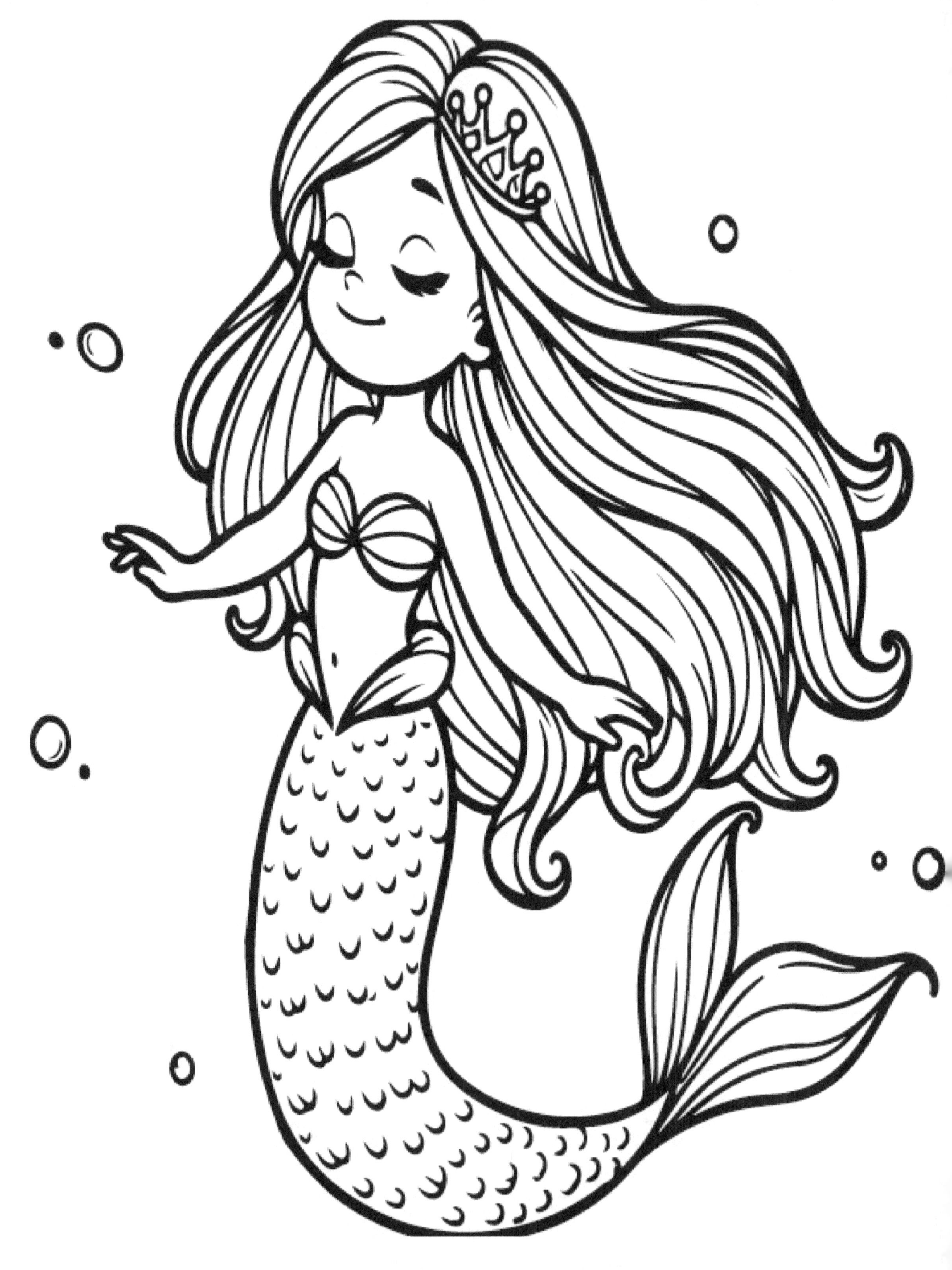

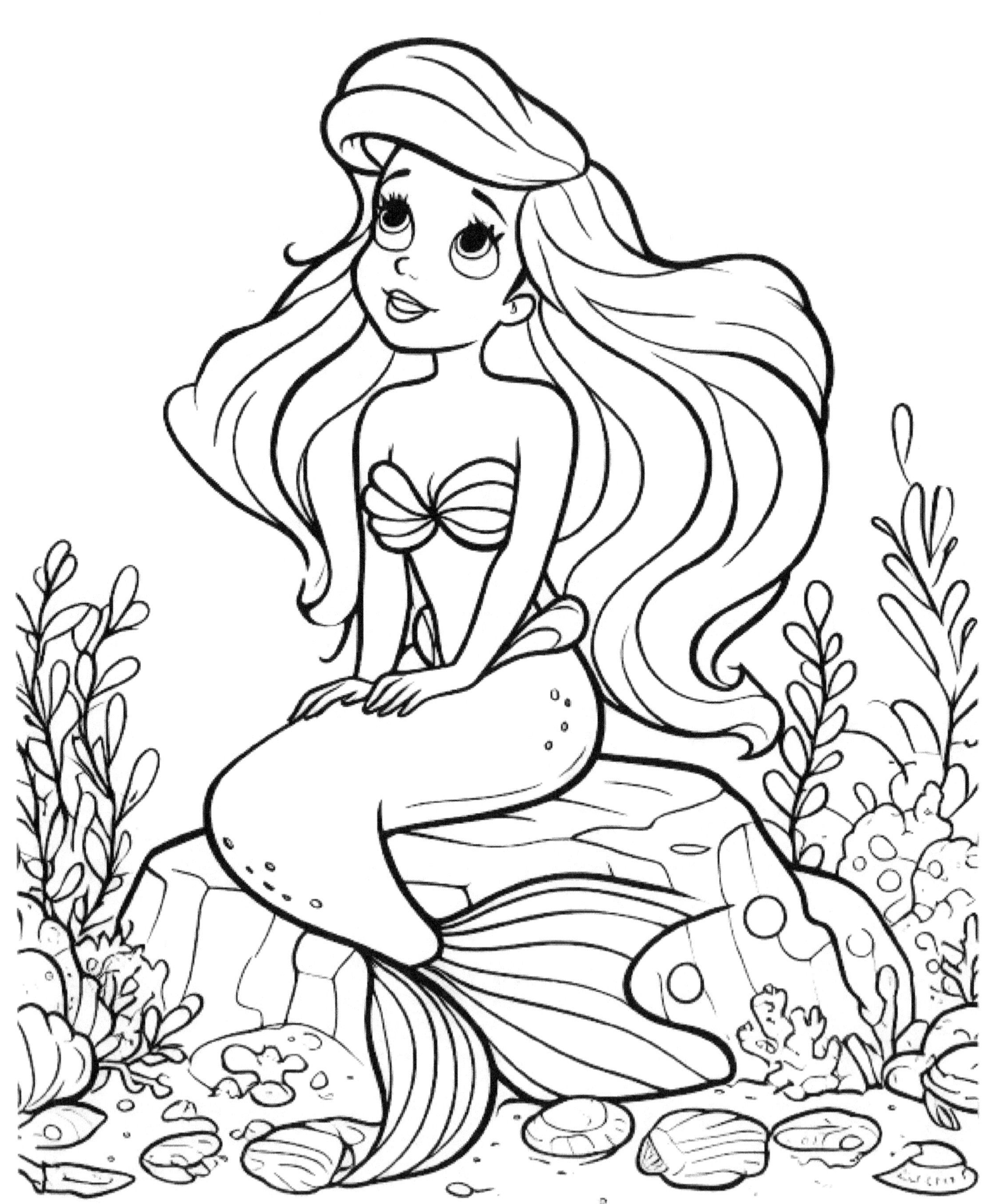

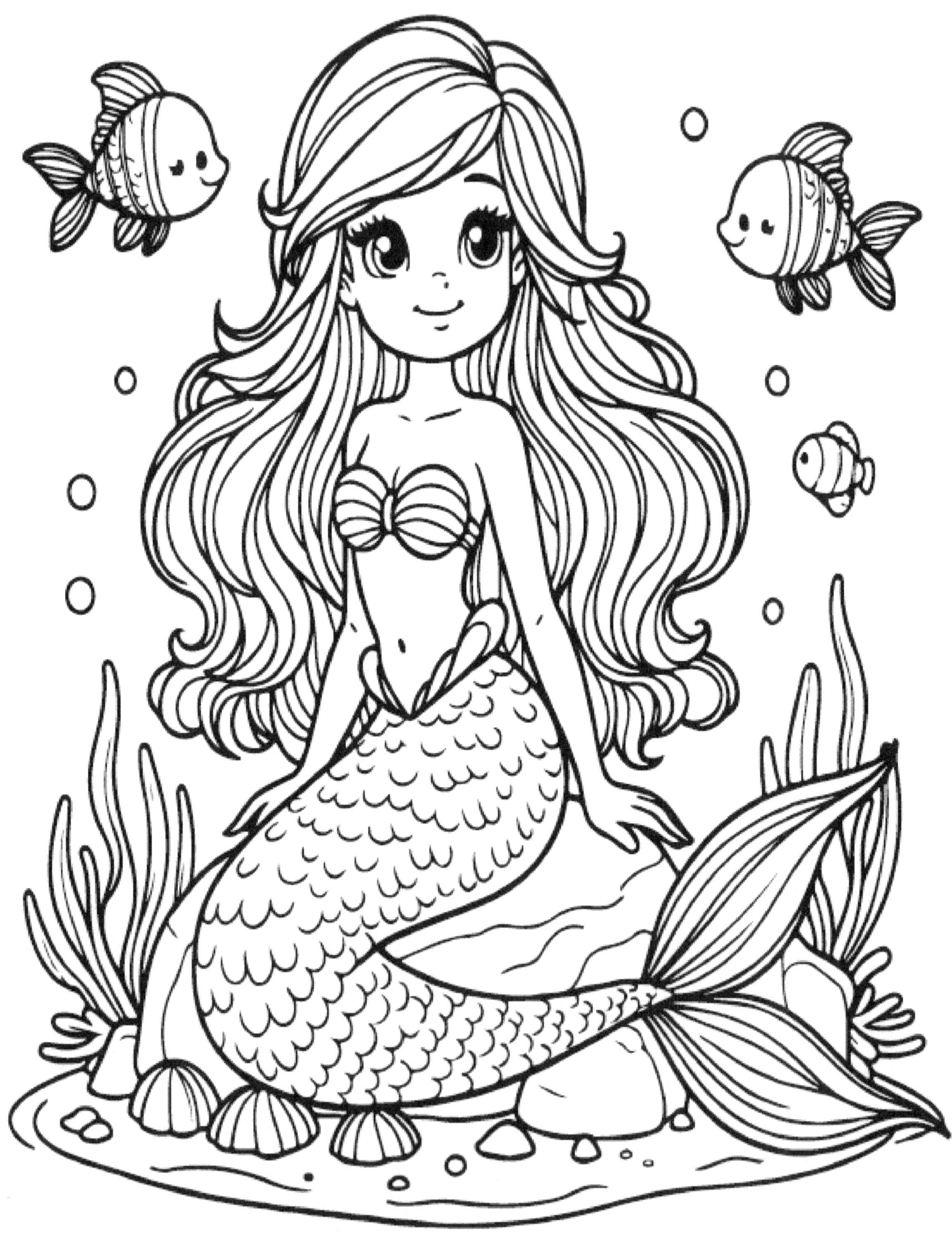

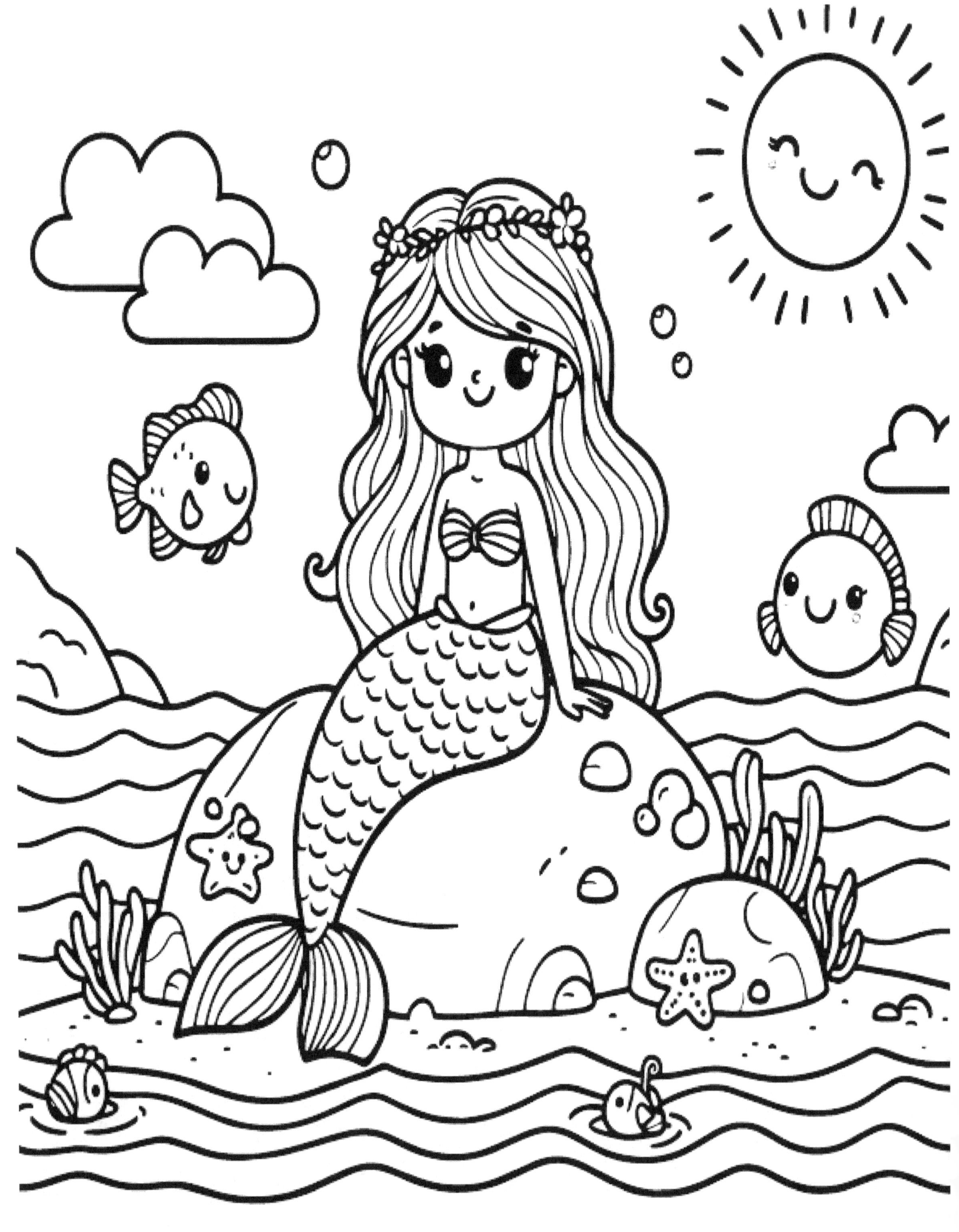

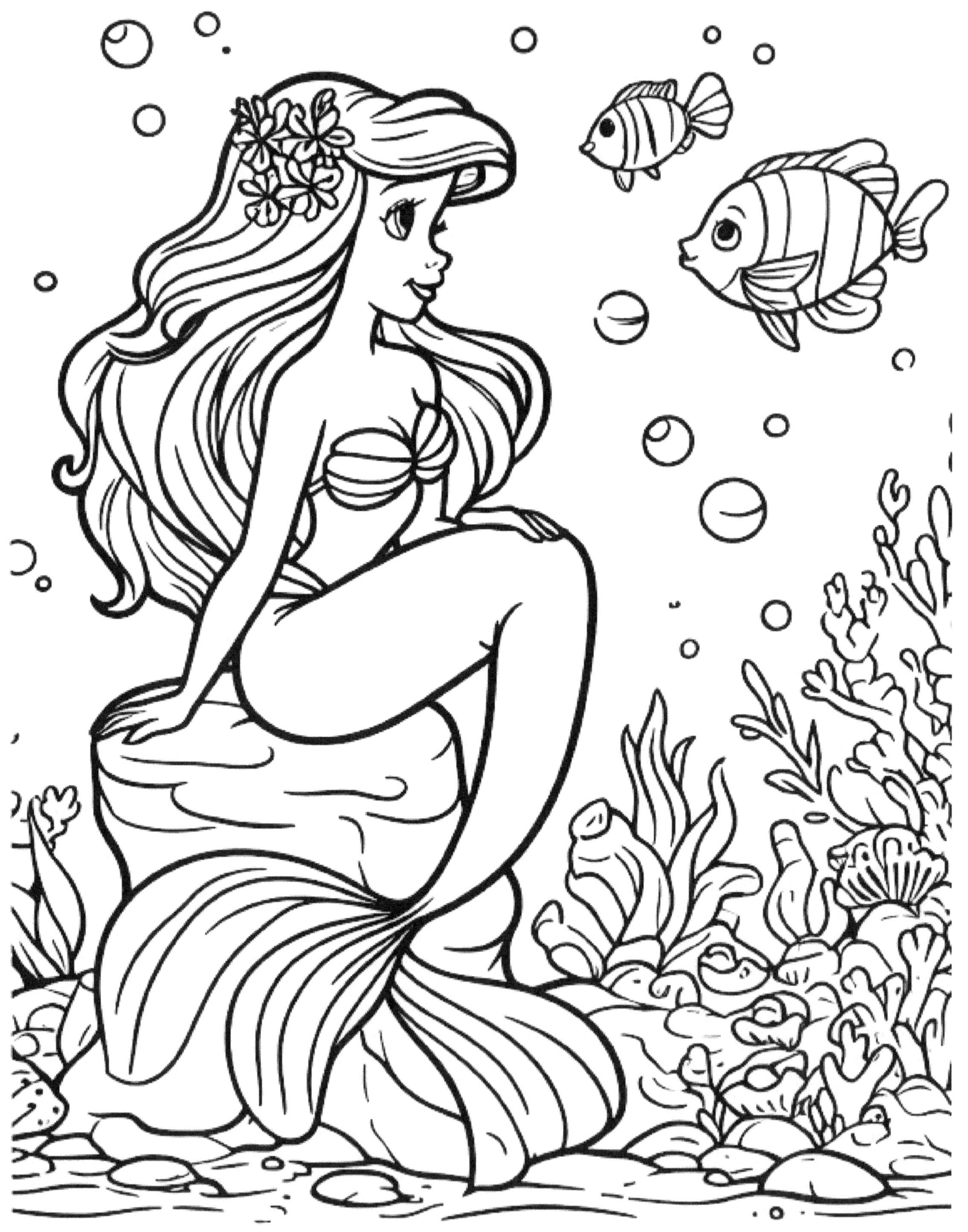

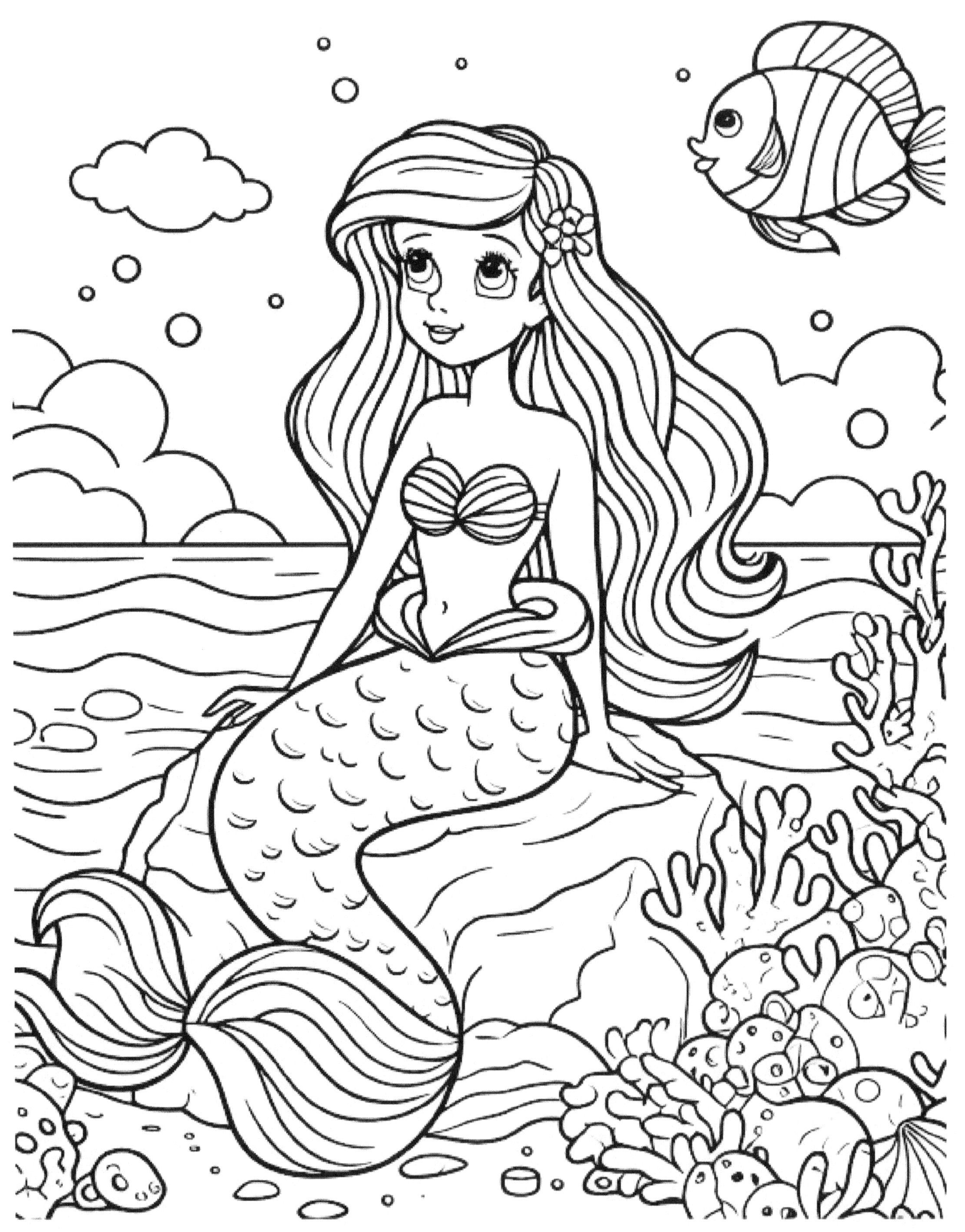

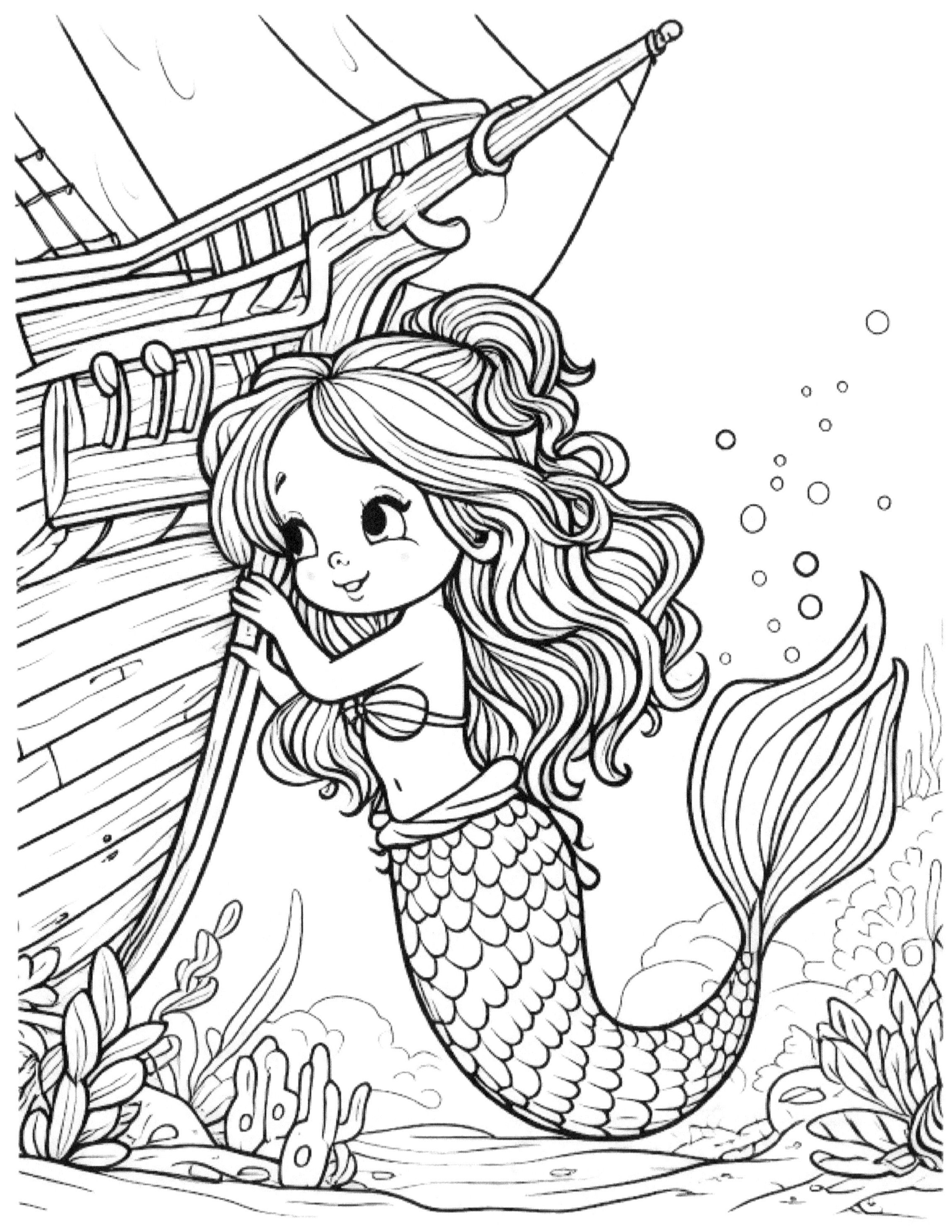

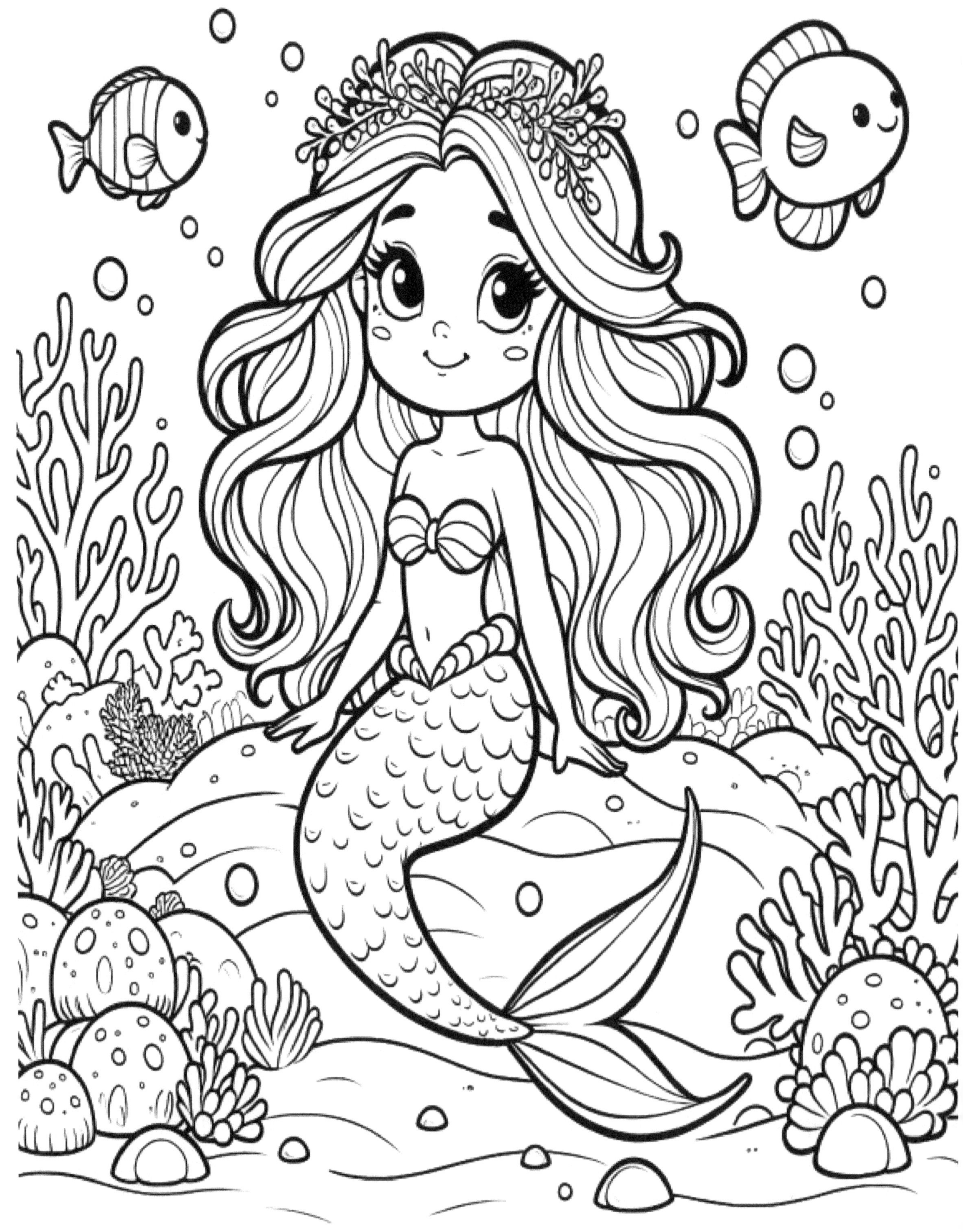

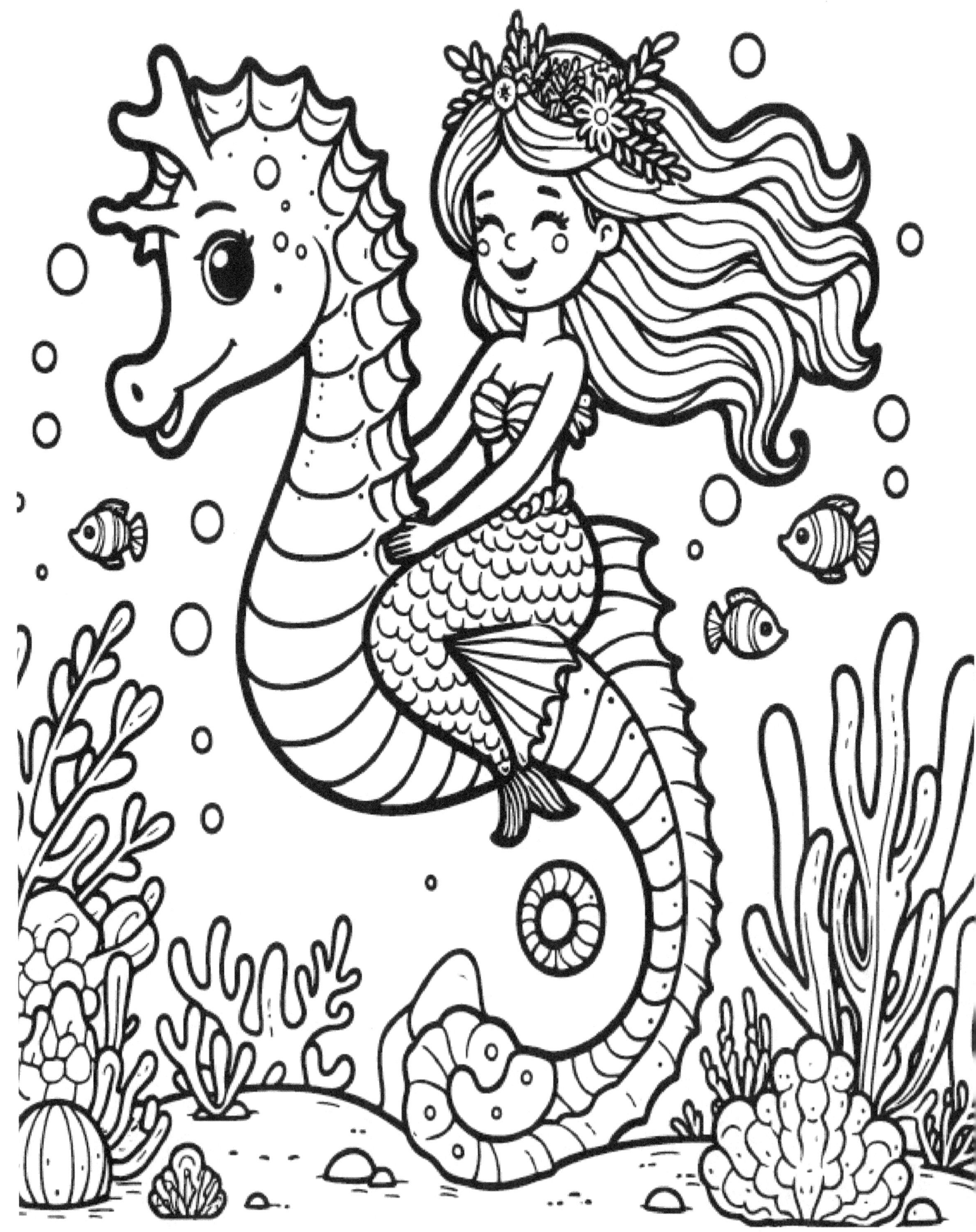

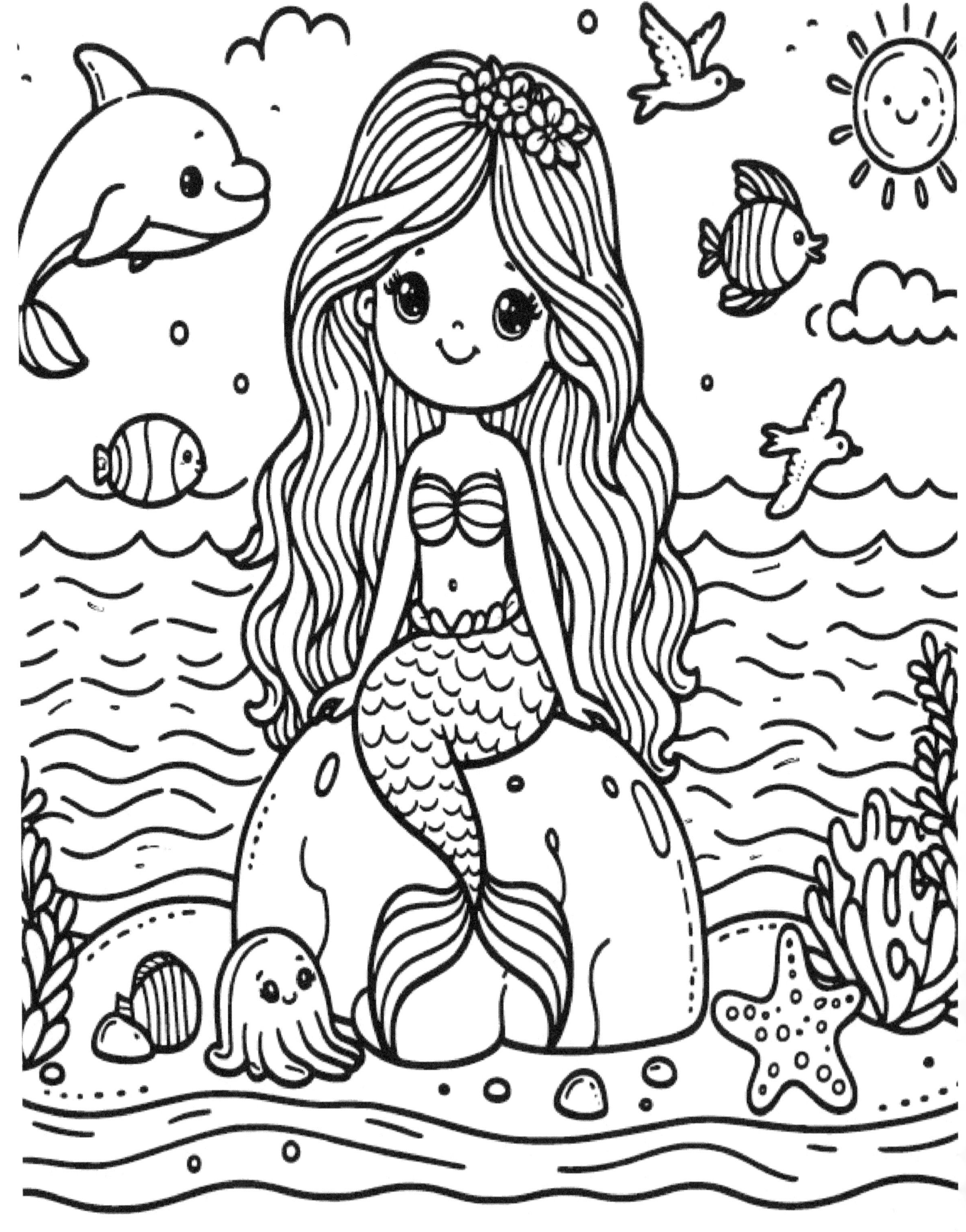

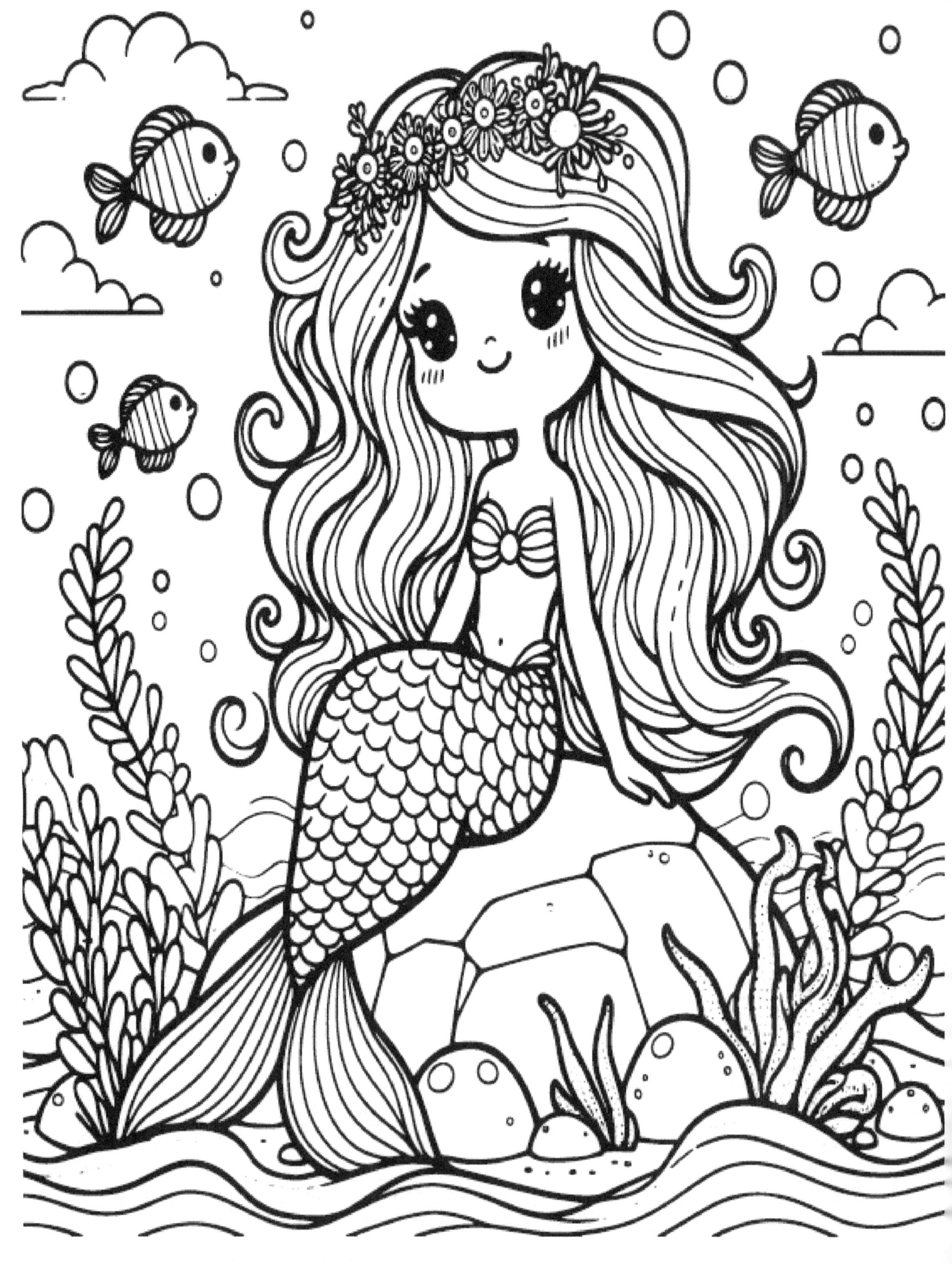

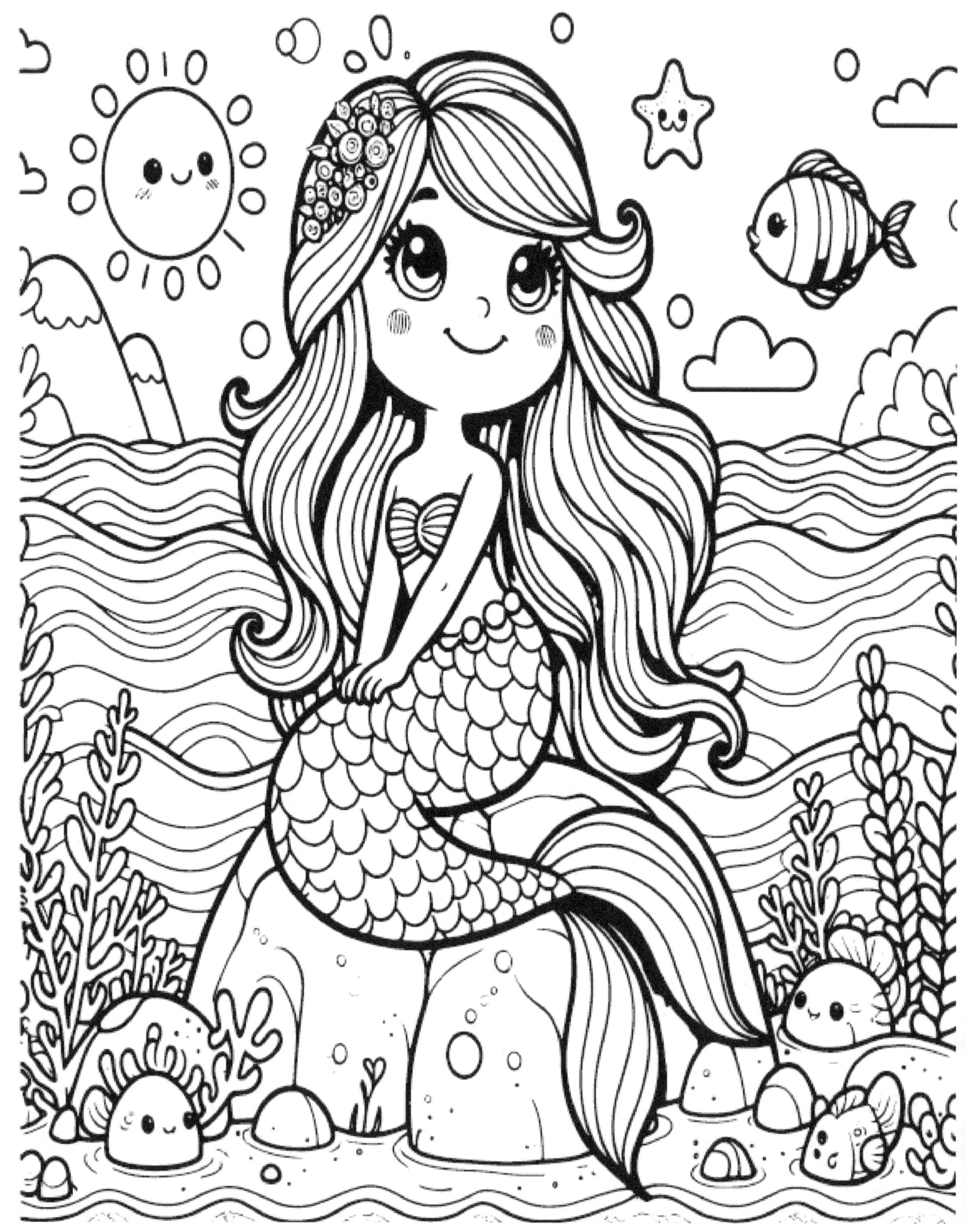

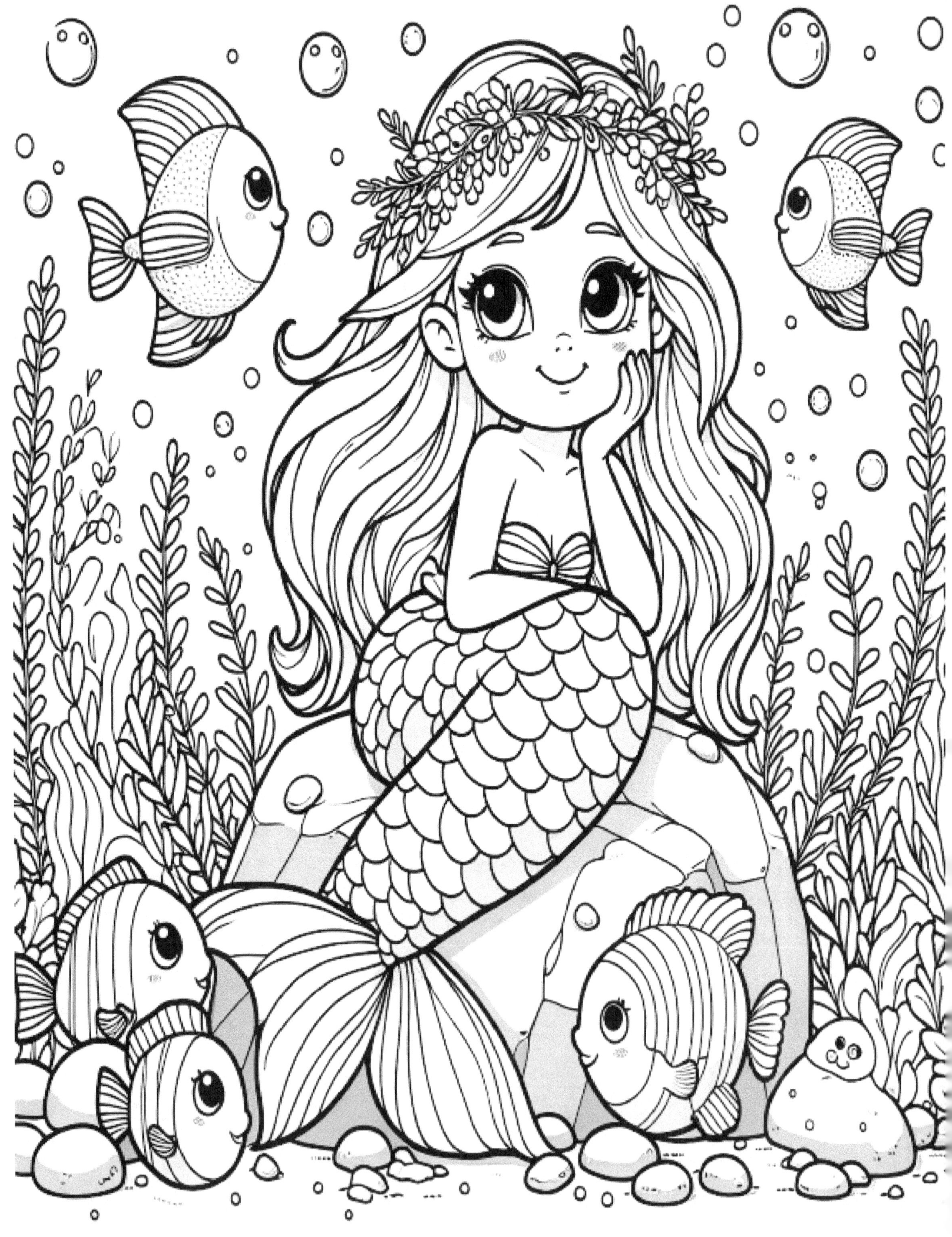

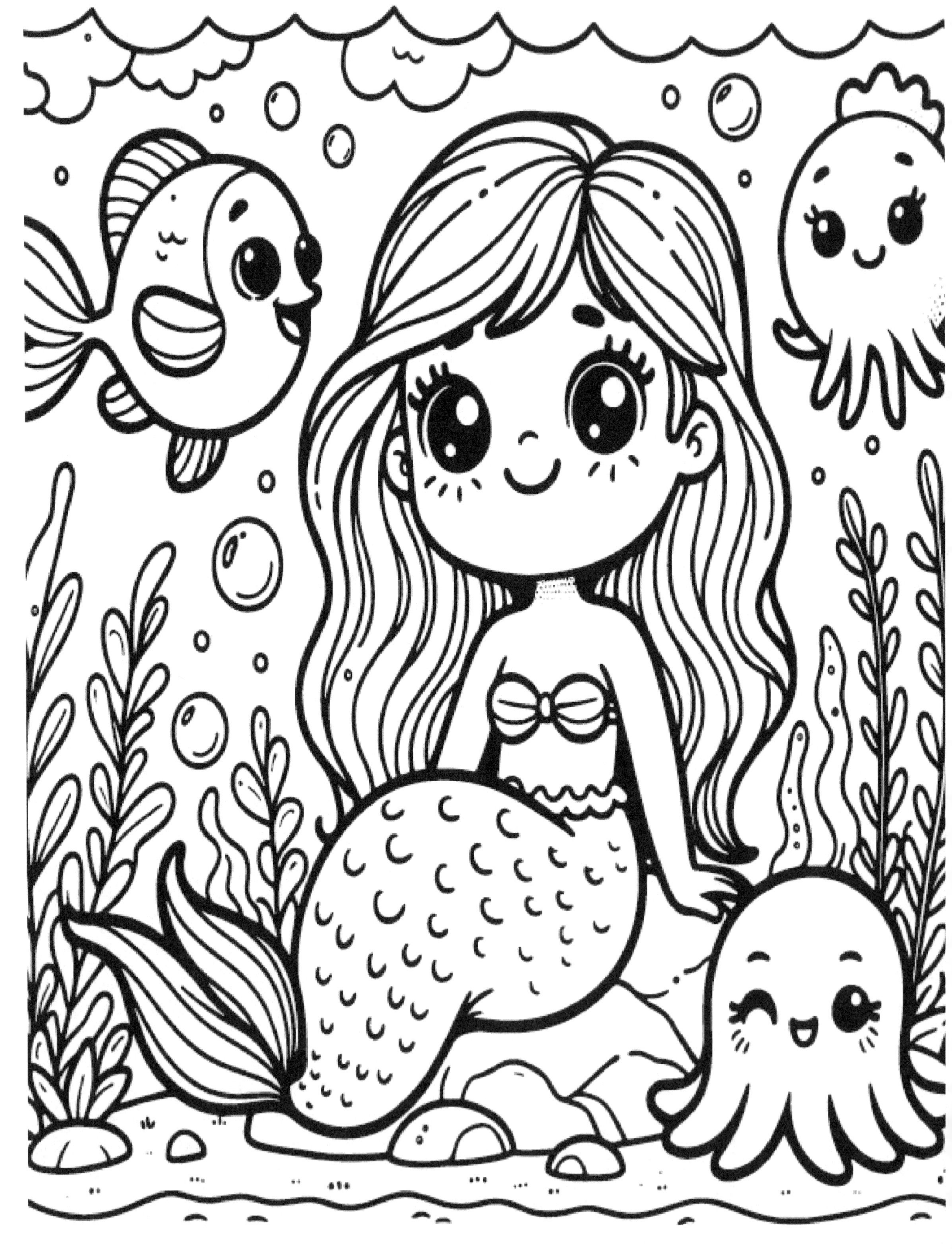

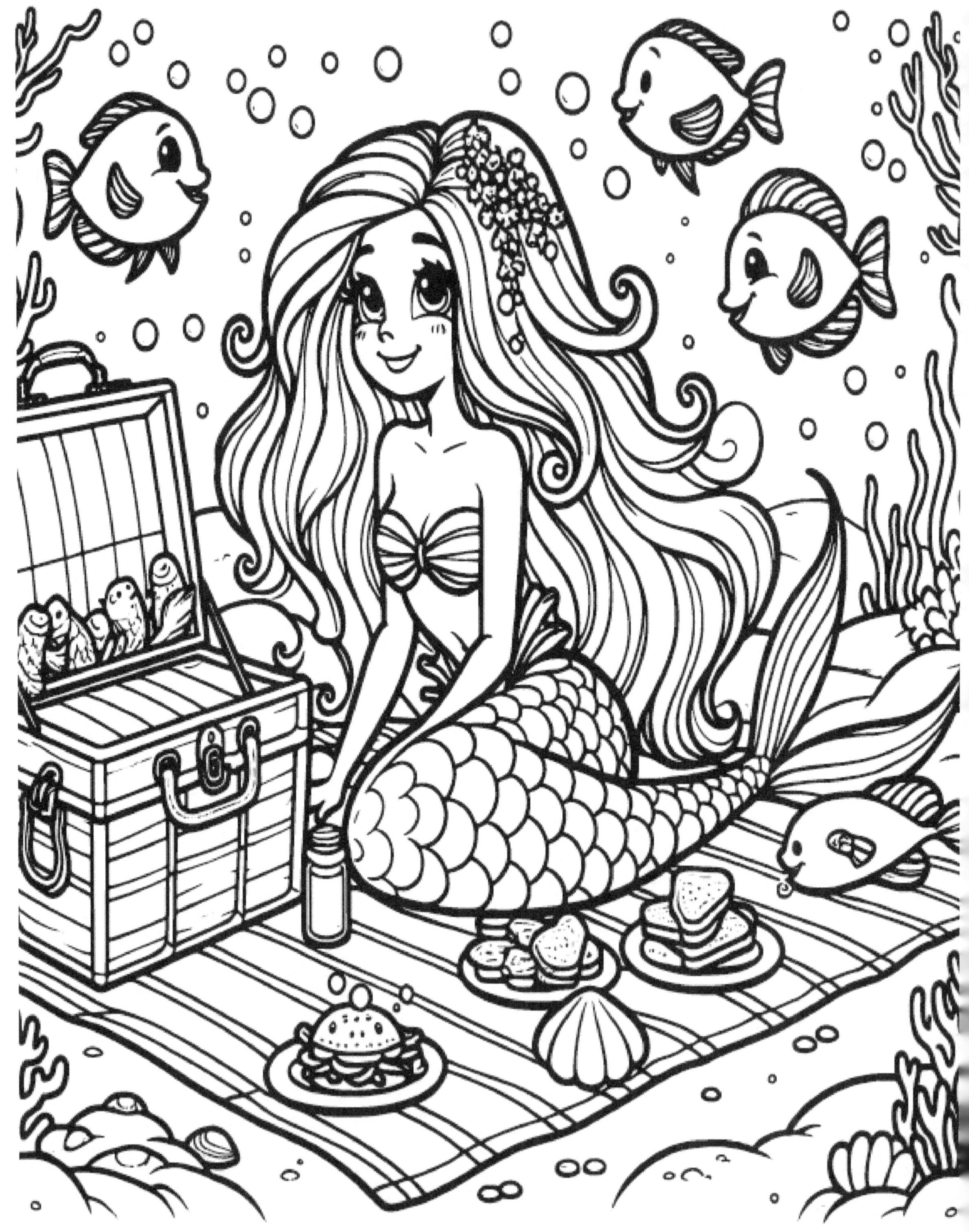

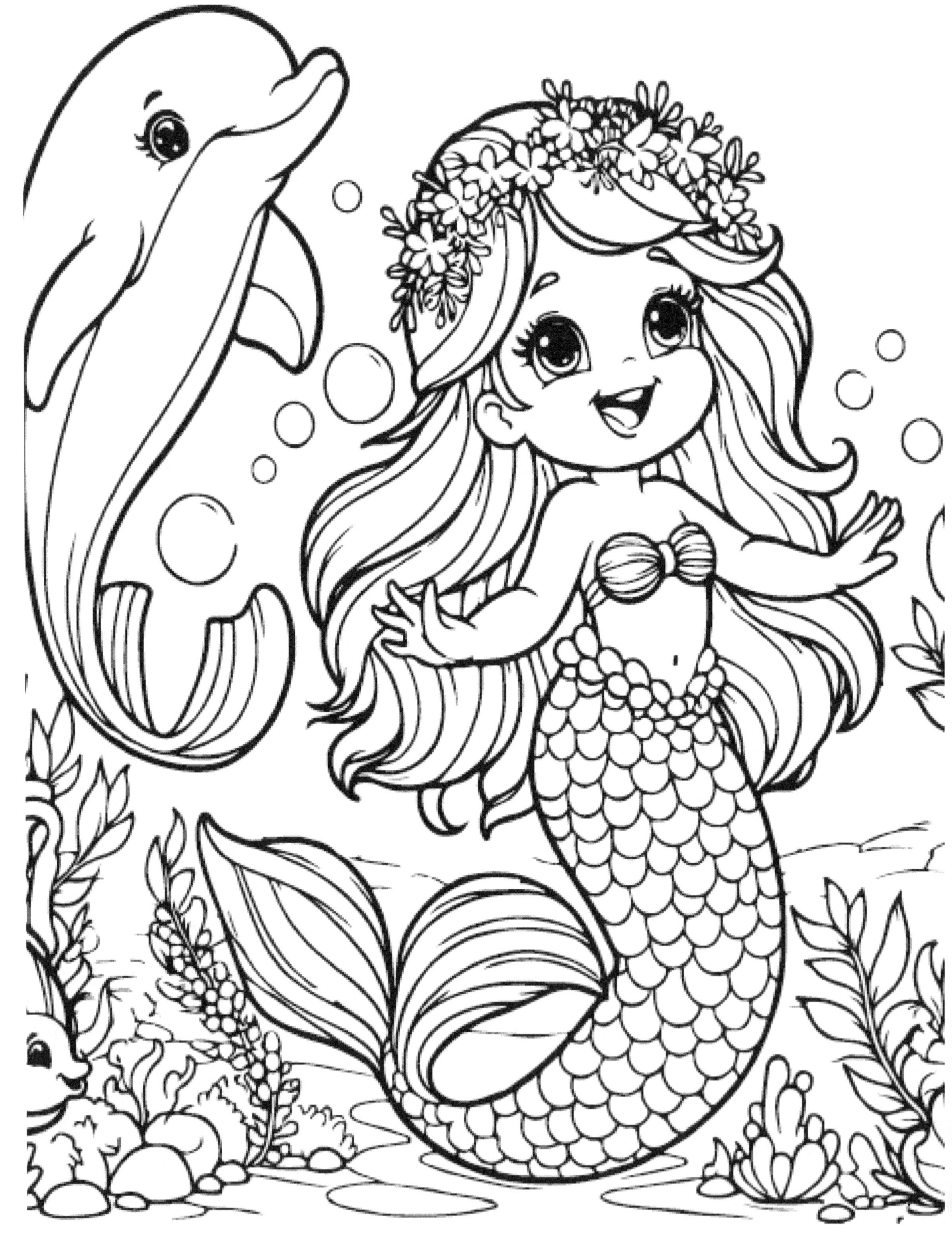

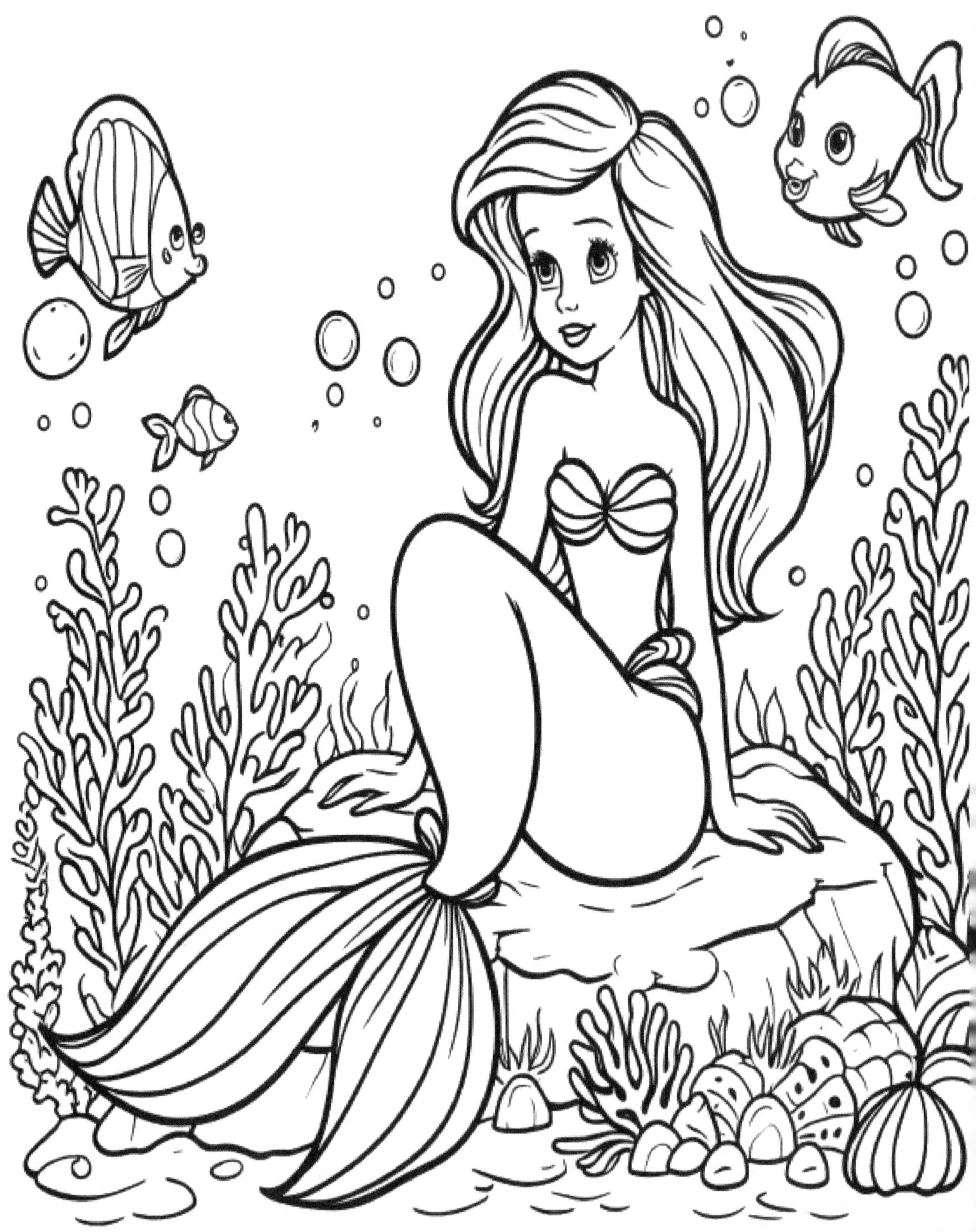

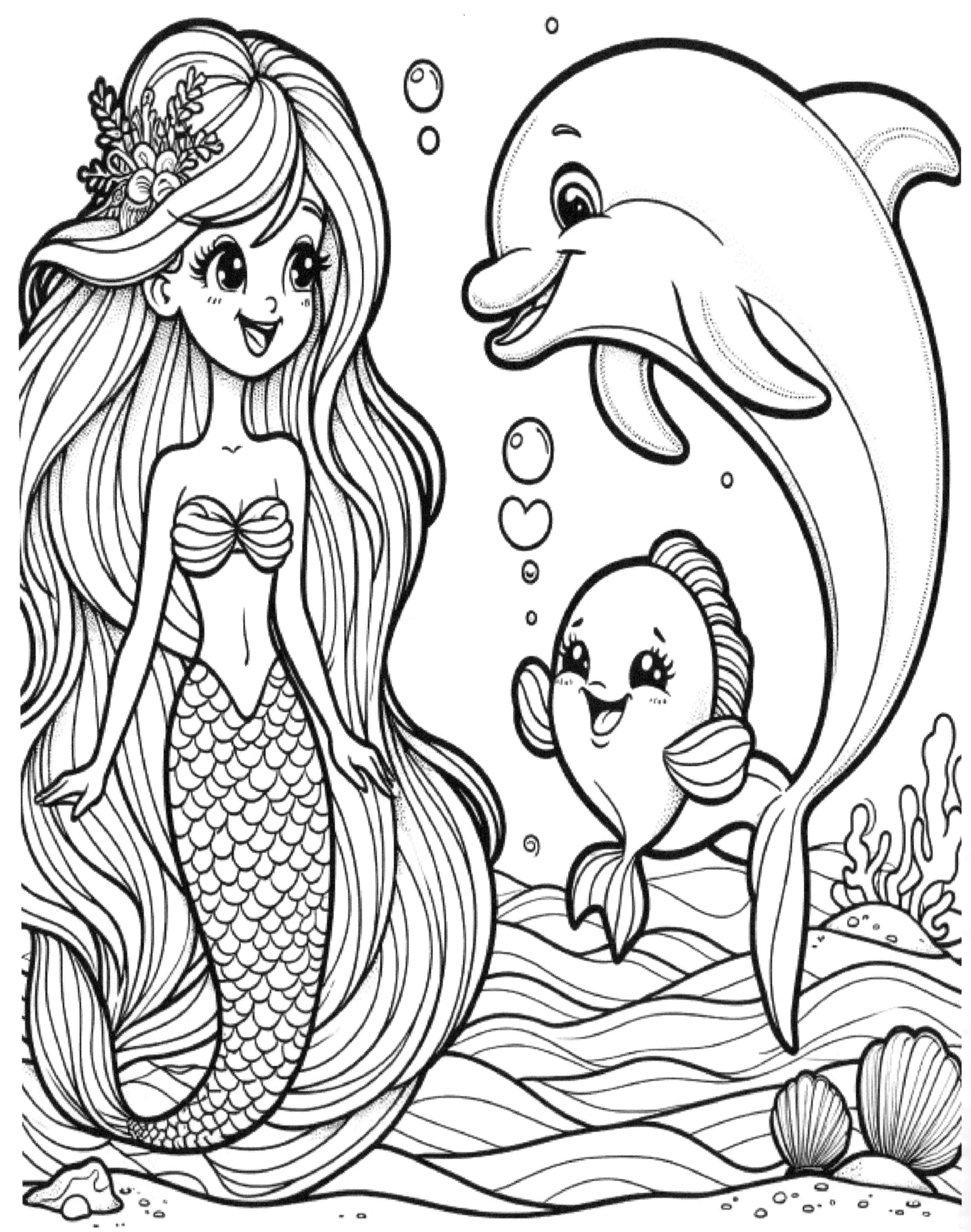

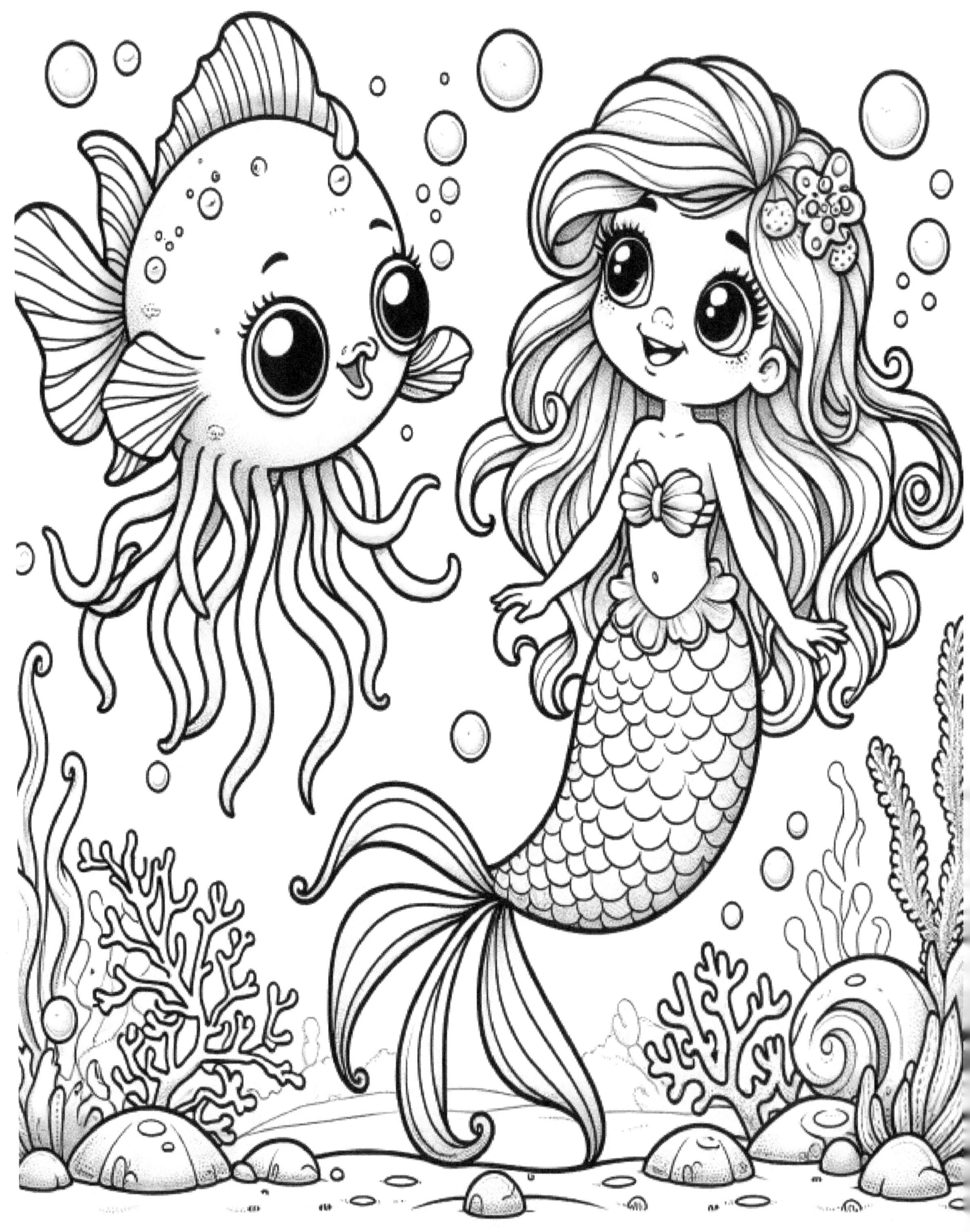

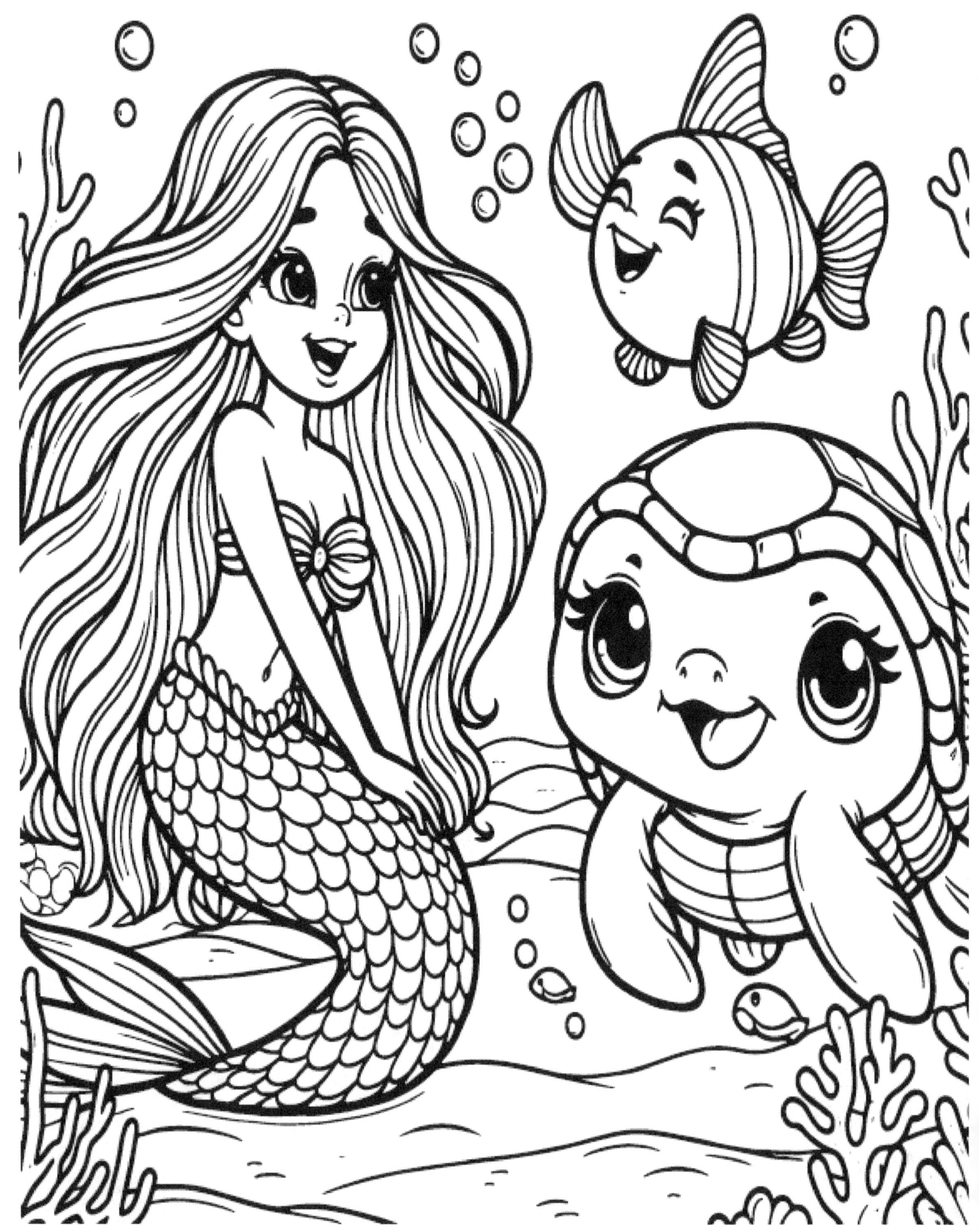

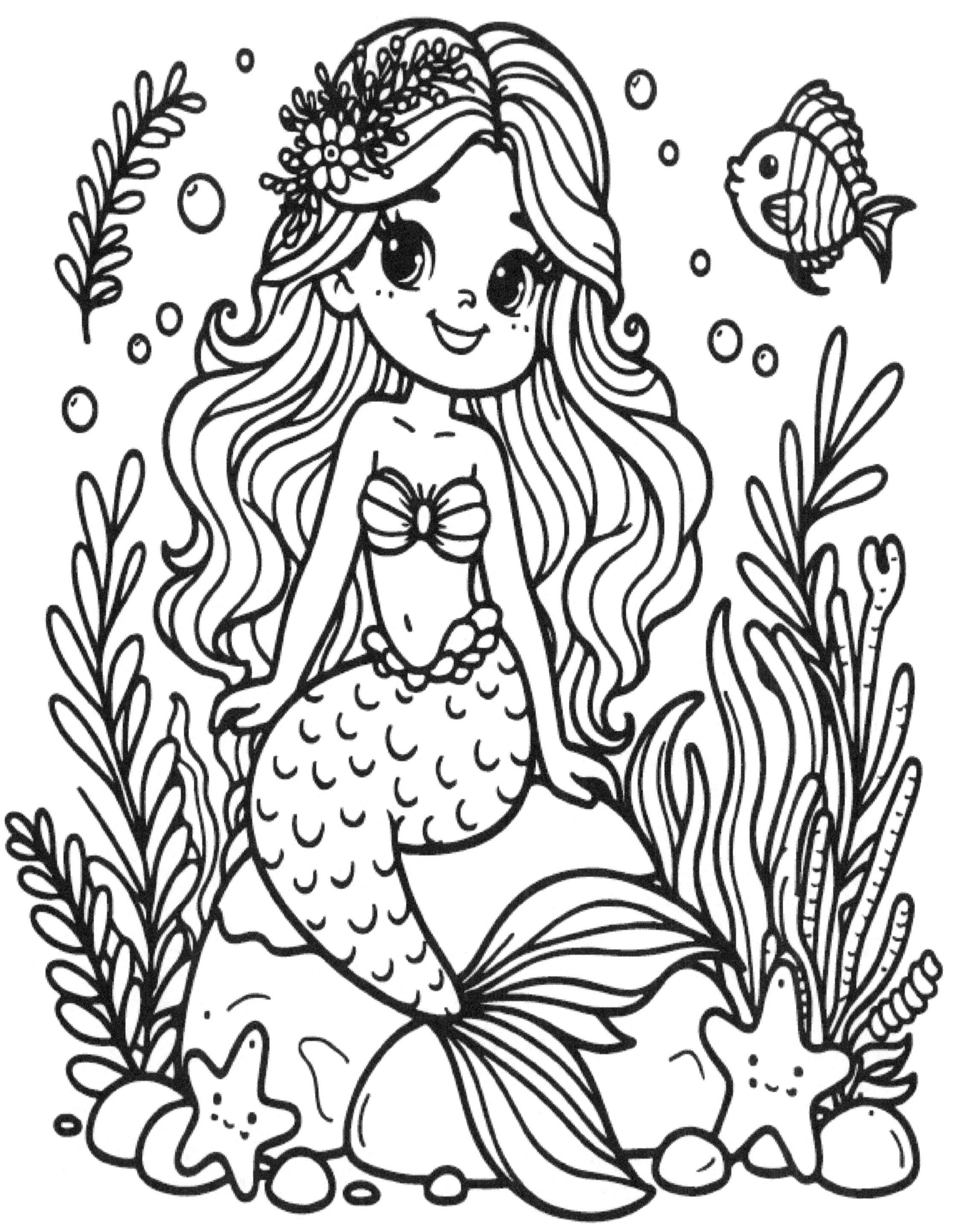

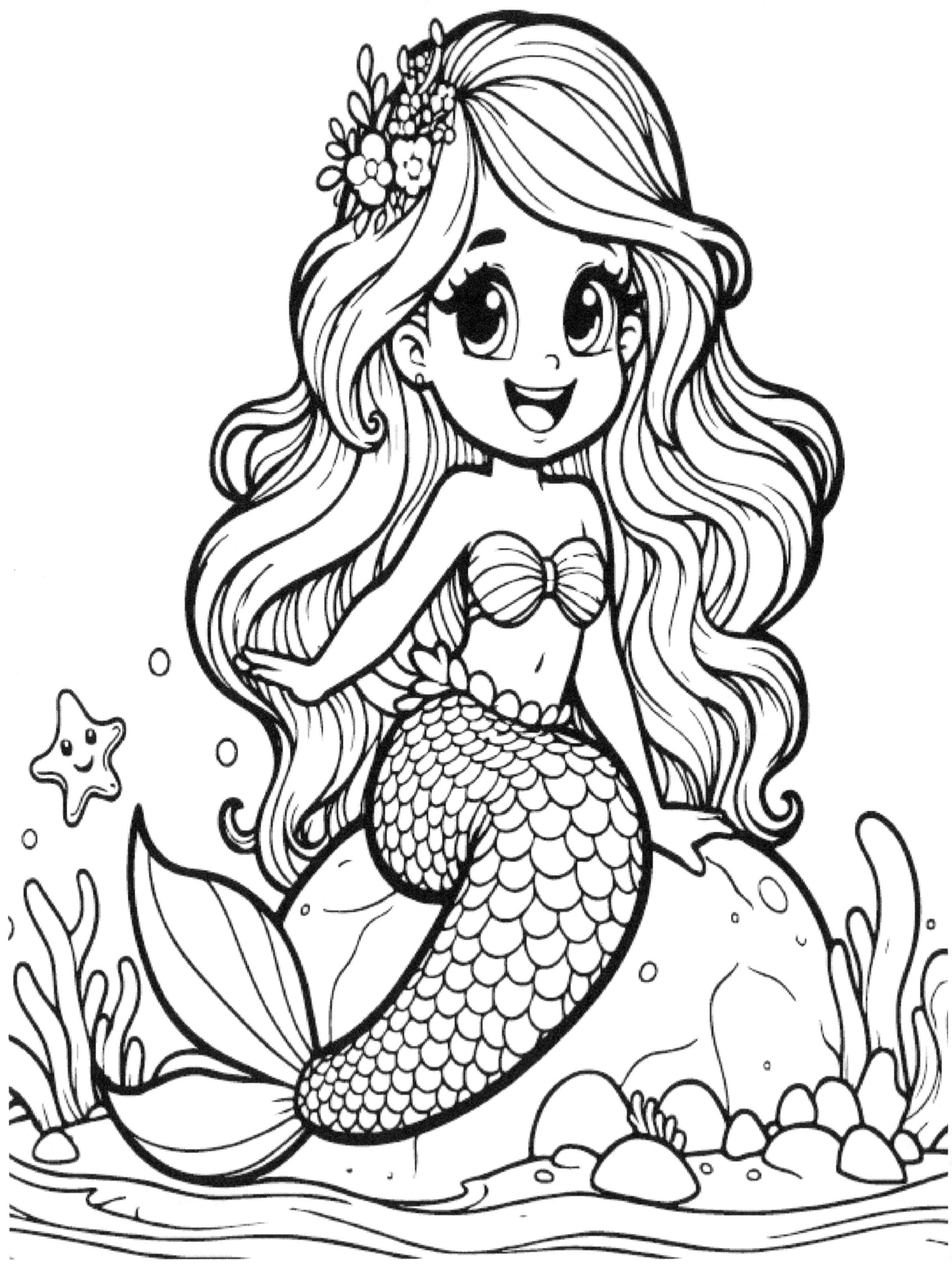

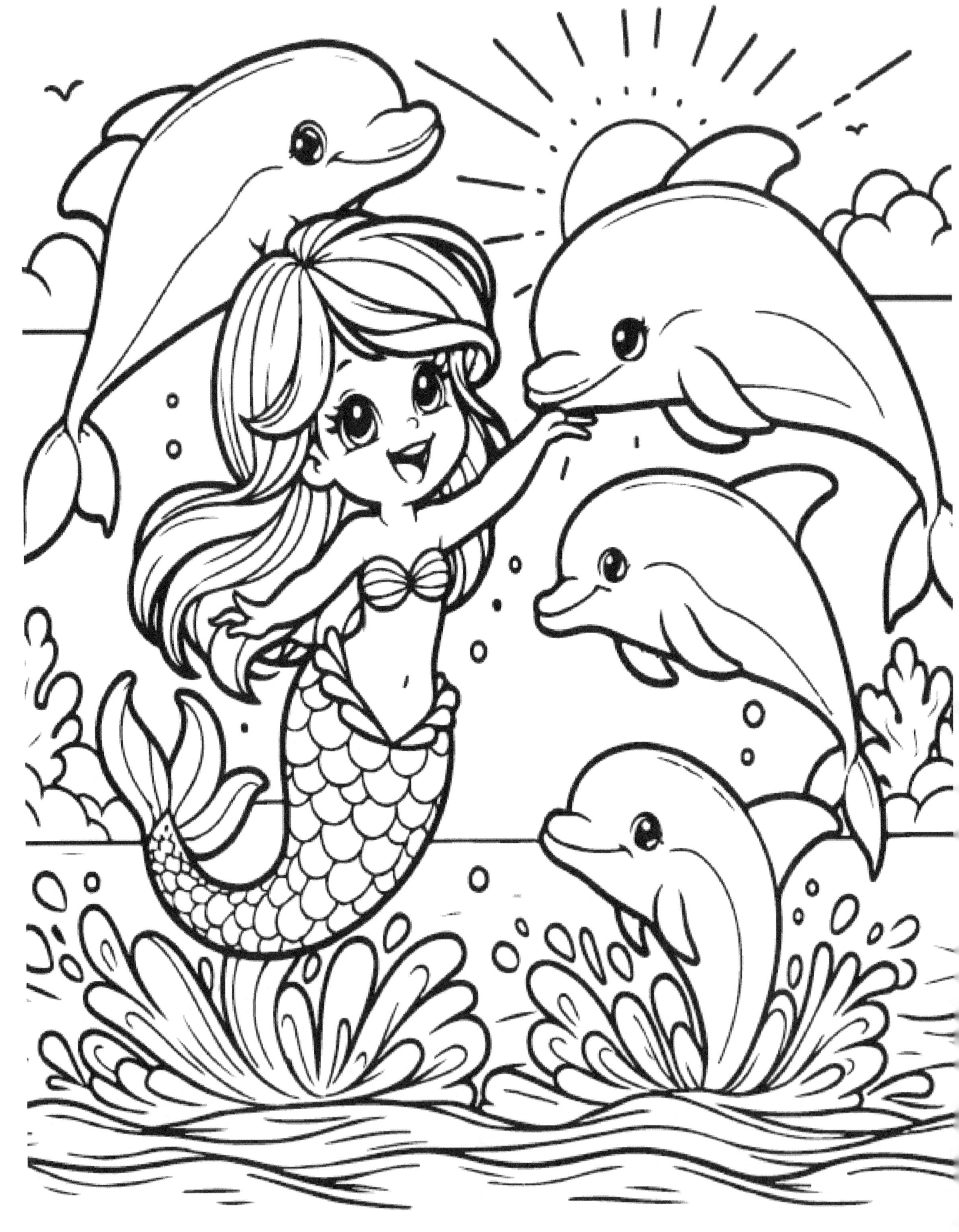

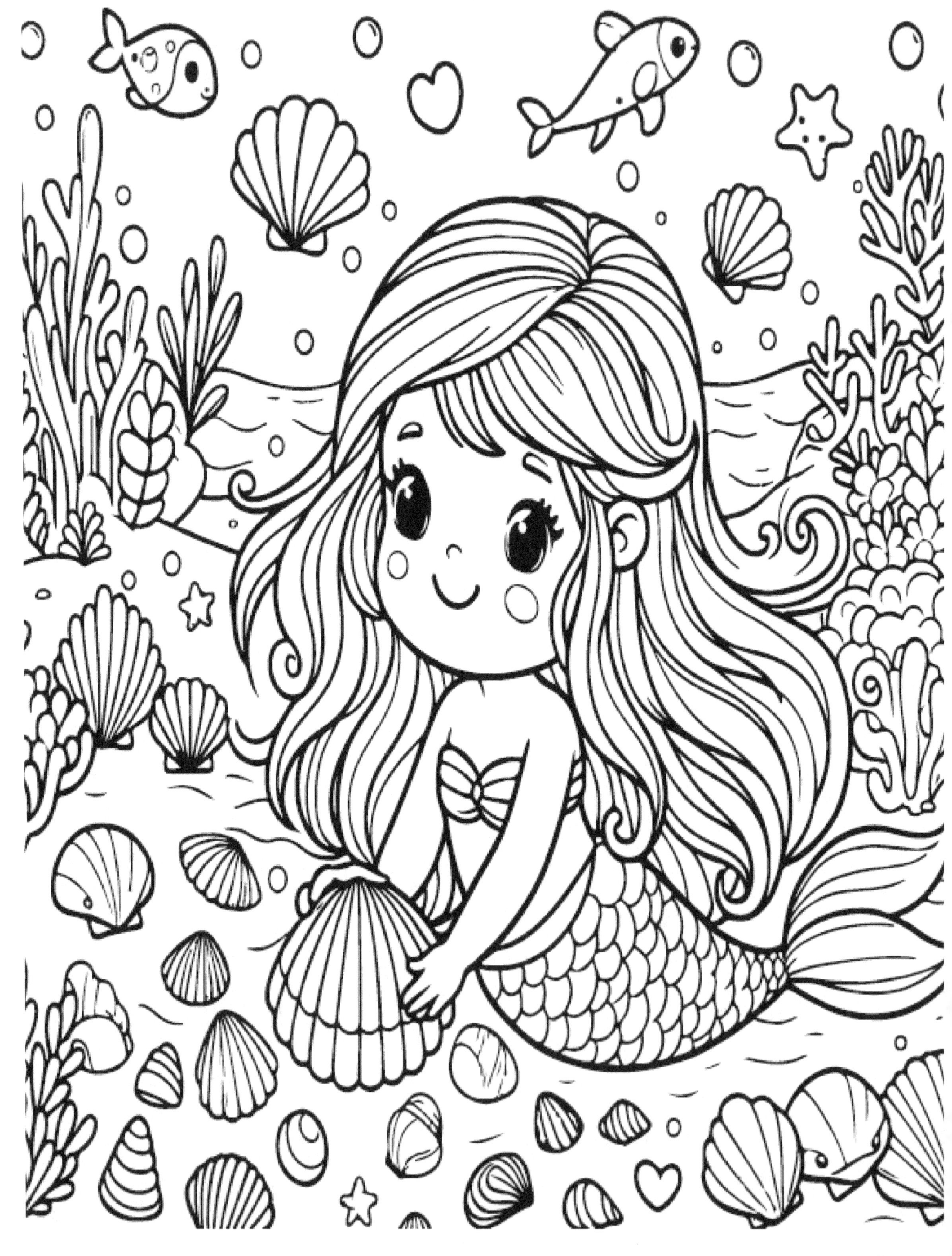

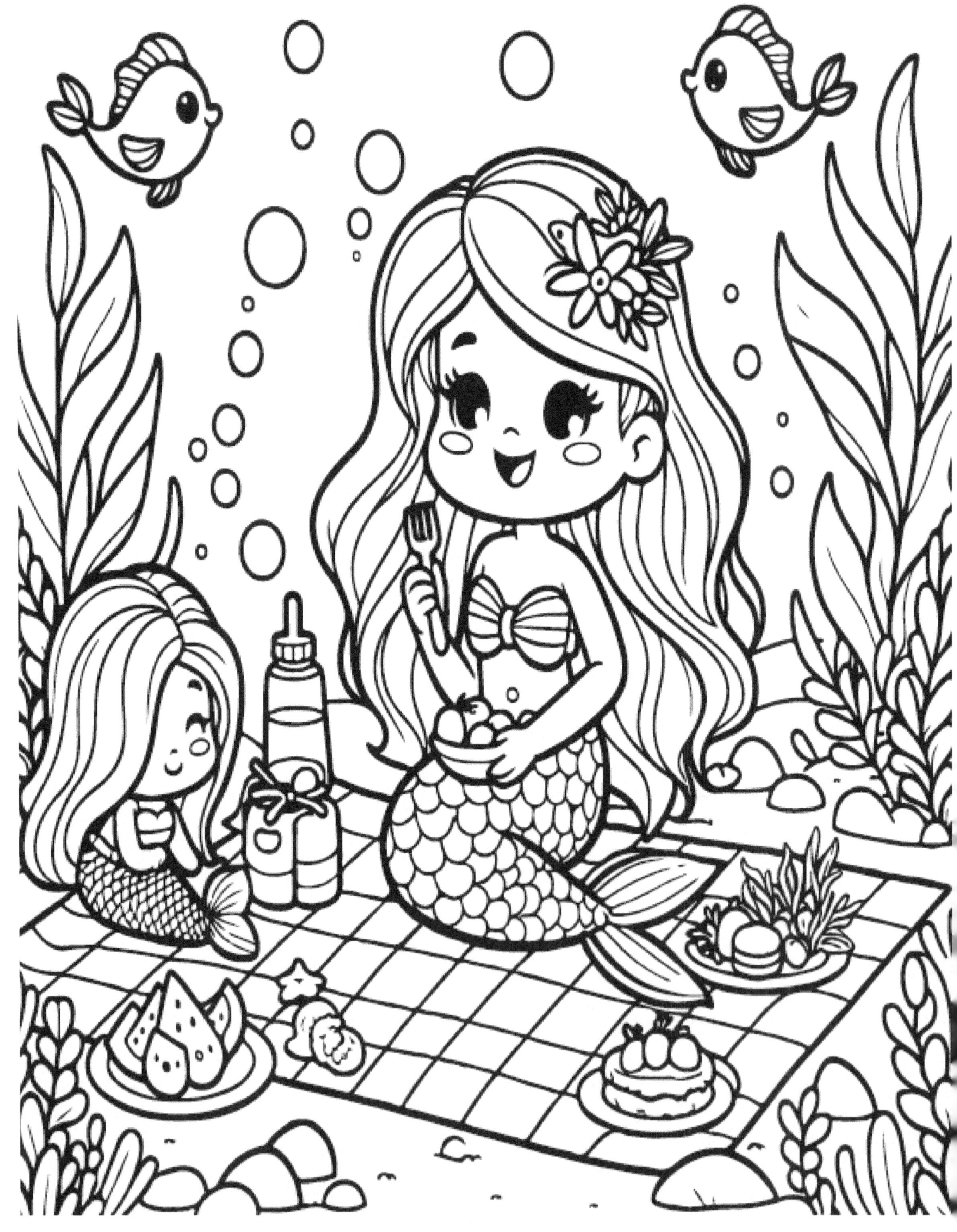

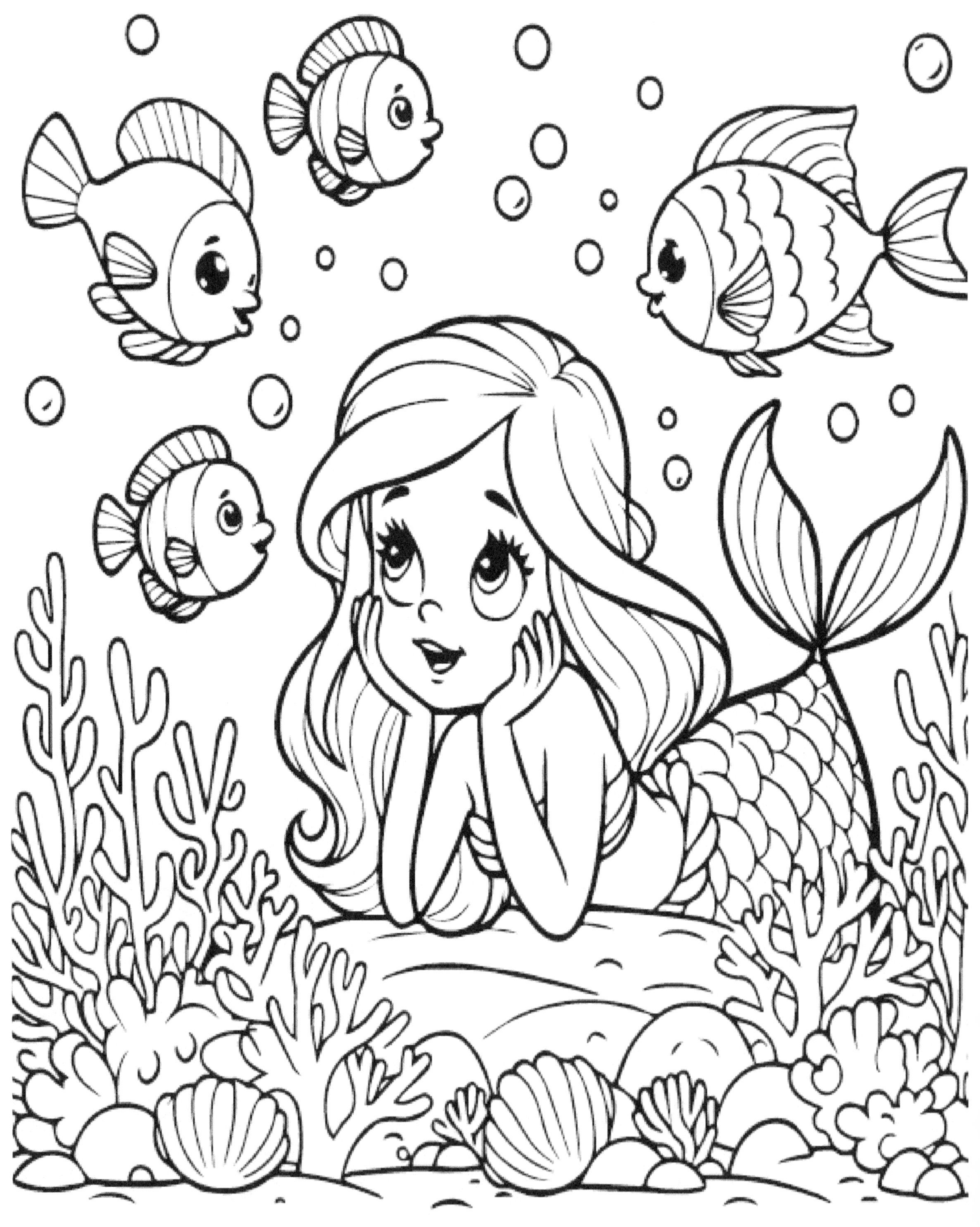

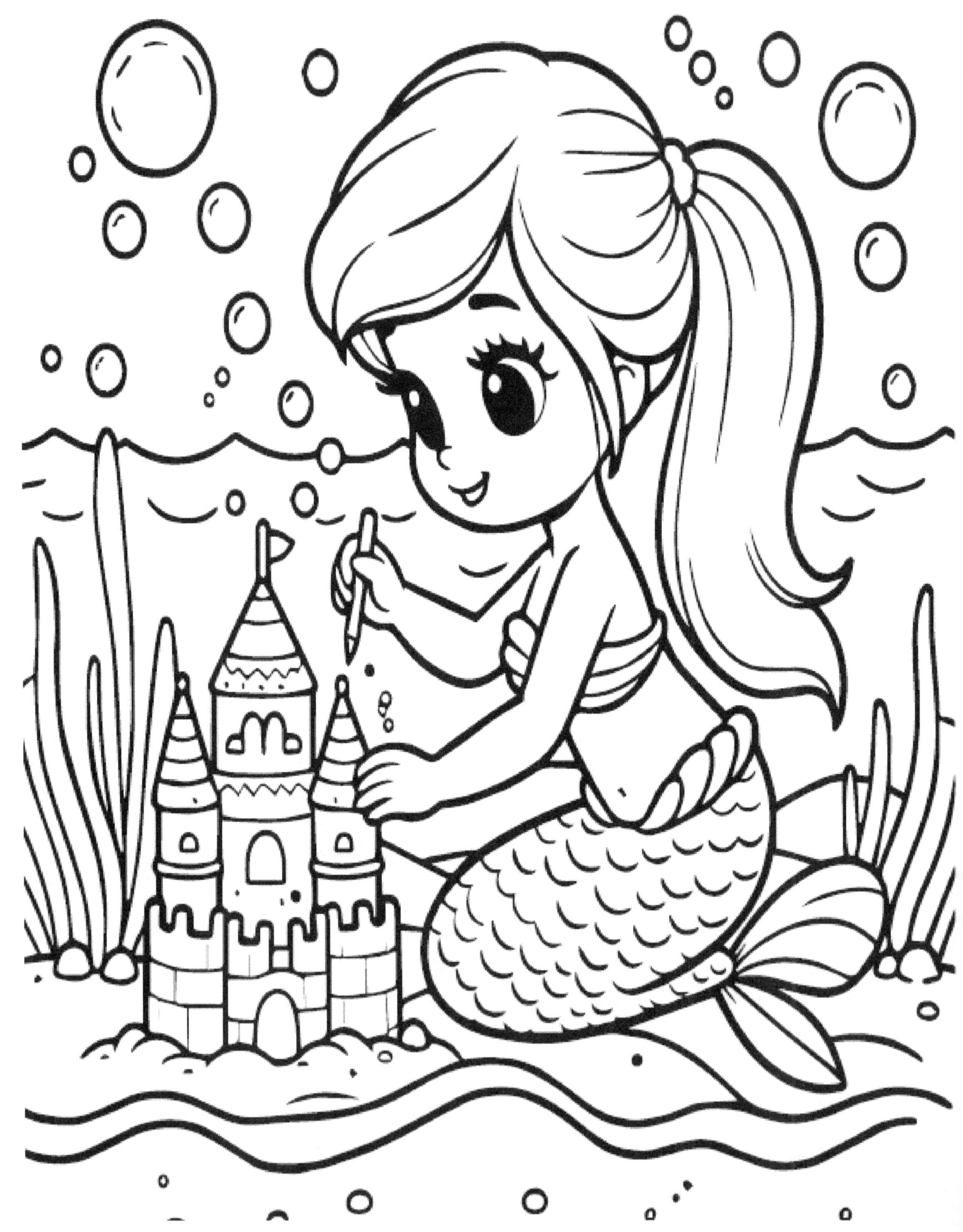

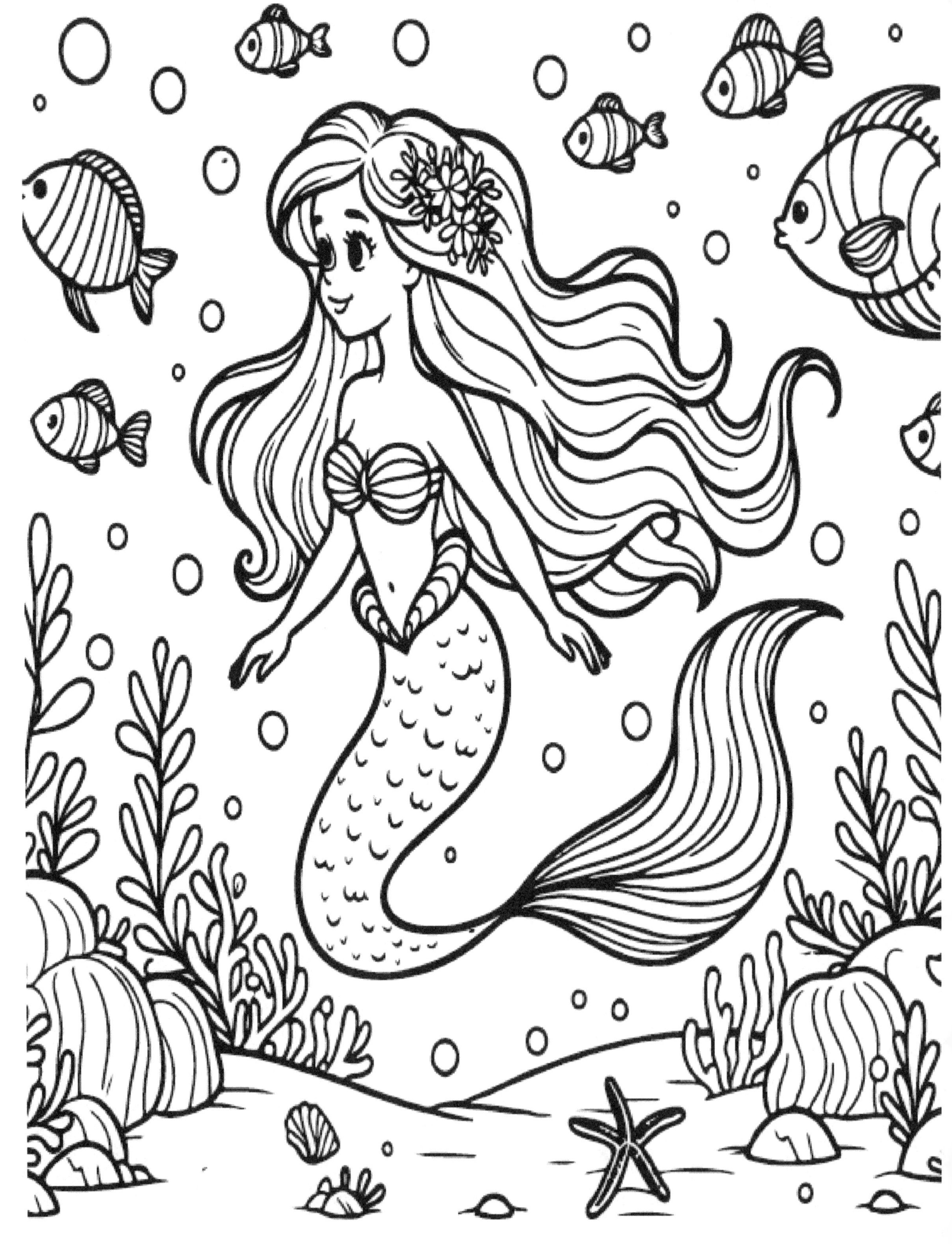

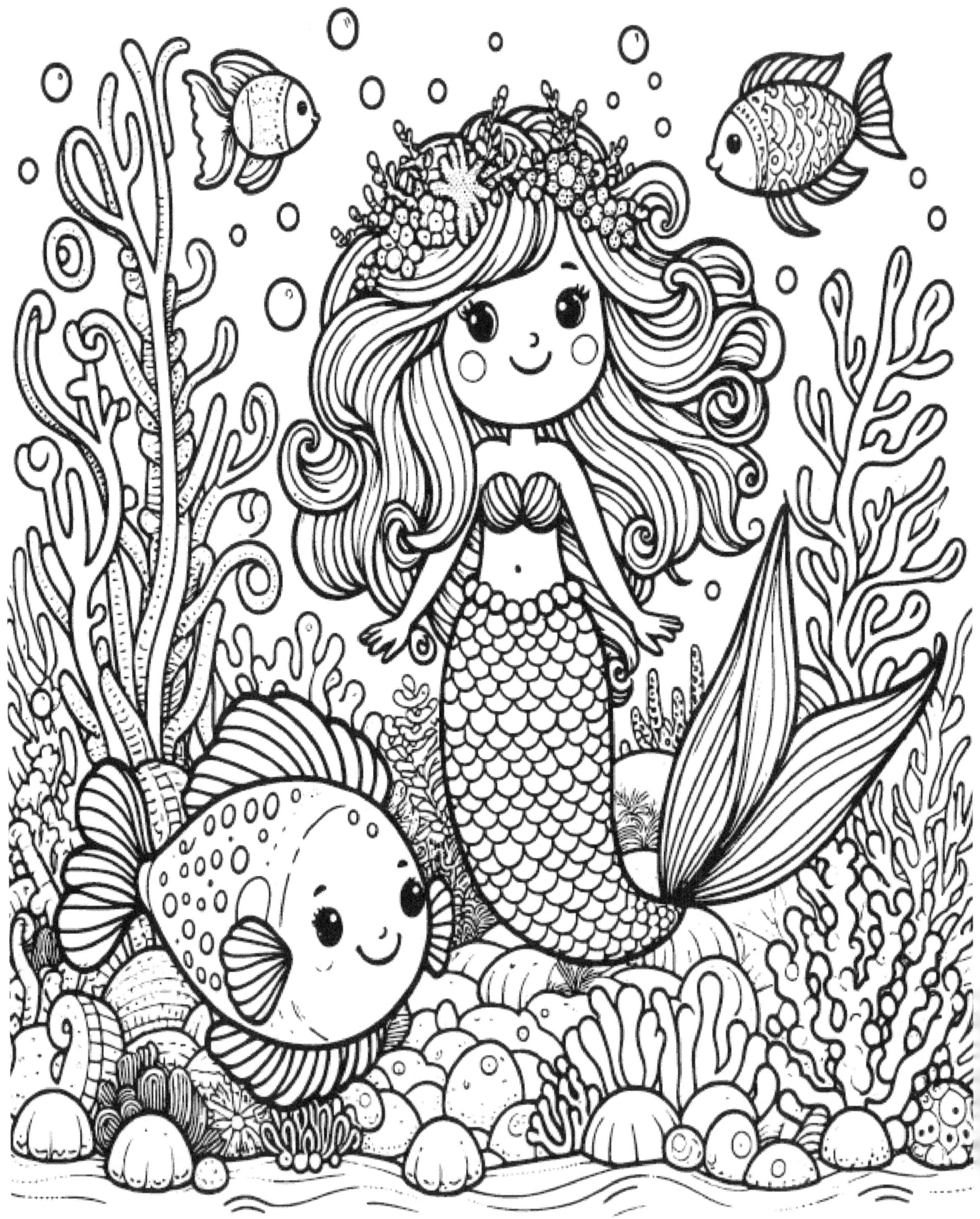